Risk Management
for Park, Recreation,
and Leisure Services

Fifth Edition

JAMES A. PETERSON
BRUCE B. HRONEK
JAMES R. GARGES

Sagamore Publishing LLC
Urbana, IL

©2008 Sagamore Publishing LLC
All rights reserved.

Publishers: Joseph J. Bannon/Peter Bannon
Production Coordinator: Laura Podeschi
Cover & Interior Design: Kenneth J. O'Brien
Graphics: Jim Hull

Library of Congress Catalog Card Number: 2007926429
ISBN: 978-1-57167-538-5
Printed in the United States

10 9 8 7 6 5 4 3

Sagamore Publishing LLC
1807 N. Federal Drive,
Urbana, IL 61801

We dedicate this book to our wives, Janice G. Peterson,
Sylvia S. Hronek, and Marty Garges. Our wives expend great effort to keep
us from "harm's way" and encourage us in all our endeavors.

Acknowledgments

The authors are indebted to the following institutions, agencies, and departments who so graciously furnished material for the appendices:

Bloomington Department of Parks and Recreation, Bloomington, IN
Champaign County Forest Preserve District, Mahomet, IL
Cleveland Metroparks, Cleveland, OH
Columbus Department of Parks and Recreation, Columbus, IN
Corpus Christi Parks and Recreation Department, Corpus Christi, TX
Foster City Department of Parks, Recreation and Vehicles, Foster City, CA
Indy Parks and Recreation, Indianapolis, IN
Iowa City Department of Parks and Recreation, Iowa City, IA
Joliet Park District, Joliet, IL
Lake County Forest Preserve District, Libertyville, IL
Long Beach Department of Parks, Recreation and Marine, Long Beach, CA
Maryland-National Capital Park and Planning Commission, Silver Springs, MD
Monmouth County Park System, Lincroft, NJ
St. Louis County Parks, St. Louis, MO
St. Paul, Minnesota Division of Parks and Recreation, St. Paul, MN

In addition, we acknowledge the cooperation of the Department of Recreation, Park, and Tourism Studies at Indiana University, Bloomington, IN, without whose support and encouragement the writing of this book would have been most difficult.

Preface

This book is intended to be a primer in risk management, tort liability, and negligence for persons working or studying in the park, recreation, and leisure services field. It is aimed at recreation professionals, volunteer leaders, university students, and members of citizen boards or commissions. The basic principles of law expressed in this book apply to local, state, and federal agencies as well as private providers of recreation. There may be a few local exceptions; therefore, the reader is cautioned to inquire as to specific variances in tort law that may exist locally.

> **Consultation with an organization's legal counsel, such as the city attorney offices, county attorney's offices, state attorney general offices, solicitors, and offices of general counsel is important in protecting you and your organization's interests.**

The purpose of this book is to develop an awareness of legal liability among leisure service providers and to aggressively take the lead in managing risk within their organizations. In addition, risk management provides a method for offering quality leisure experiences with maximum protection for participants and adequate safeguards under the law for leaders, administrators, and organizations offering the recreation services. It is important to note that *a good public safety program is good public policy*.

A good risk-management plan should be designed first and foremost to allow participants a quality experience in a safe surrounding. The plan should also include provisions to protect service providers and their employees from undue risk. *A good risk-management program does not cost, it saves.* A risk-management program should concentrate on providing the visitor to the recreation facility a safe experience. When an organization makes an effort to protect the visitor the bonus results will include a reduction in the potential of successful civil lawsuits.

The trend toward increased litigation and the willingness to sue over rather trivial matters make this book particularly applicable to the recreation and leisure service practitioner.

Recreation organizations and individuals are encouraged to adapt any of the information in this book to meet the specific needs of their departments or agencies. Each legal jurisdiction applies negligence laws in a slightly different manner; therefore, it is important that you *check with your legal counsel before proceeding with legal issues and processes*. While some forms and checklists may be suitable in their present form, not all may be applicable.

This book is intended as an aid for handling risk. It is not intended to be a substitute for legal counsel, actuarial assistance, or other professional services. *Some enclosed forms and specifications may be inappropriate or inaccurate for your jurisdiction.* The text is kept intentionally brief, simple, and as free of "legalese" as possible so that all readers may gain a healthy respect and appreciation for tort liability. Where cited, cases will be as current as possible, using cases that have been tried in the appellate courts. It is not the intent of the authors to use sensational cases that are the exception to general court rulings.

Introduction

Why Risk Management?

Parks padlocked! Police patrol to keep people from selling drugs to children in parks! Playground equipment moved because of the threat of lawsuits! Park buildings covered with graffiti! Who would have thought a few years ago that park and recreation systems throughout the country would be forced to close some of their operations during part of the day, for weeks, or permanently because of risk considerations? Who would have guessed that one reason would be the high cost of insurance premiums and dangers to their users because of high crime rates? A risk management program is no longer a luxury . . . it is a necessity for the survival of private and public recreation and leisure service providers.

A newspaper article published August 21, 2006, in the *Tampa (Florida) Tribune* accurately describes the current insurance dilemma as follows:

Tampa's decision to largely self-insure is a risky solution to the insurance crisis because the city lacks the funds that would be needed to rebuild the many buildings it owns (in case of a hurricane), including the aquarium, the convention center and city hall. Tampa mayor Pam Iorio decided to move toward self-insurance after receiving the city's latest property insurance bill. Last year the city paid $2.8 million for $500 million in property insurance coverage. This year it will pay $3.9 million for 230 million in coverage. Worse, the new insurance policy covers a maximum of $30 million in storm damage.[1]

The federal court system is an example of all court jurisdictions when it comes to the heavy litigation activity that plagues the courts. A hundred years ago the United States was named in 2,500 cases (both civil and criminal).[2] In 2005 there were more than 300,000 cases filed in federal courts.[3] The sample statistics below are replicated, more or less, in all 50 state legal systems.

As a result of Americans' propensity to sue and the high cost of effective insurance, many providers of recreation, both private and public, are either underinsured or have no insurance coverage at all. *A lack of insurance does not stop the courts from compensating injured or damaged plaintiffs.* Public agencies *must* pay court

Year	U.S. District Court Civil Cases Filed	U.S. Court of Appeals Civil Cases Filed	Authorized Judges / Cases per Panel	U.S. Criminal Cases Filed	U.S. Bankruptcy Cases Filed
2001	250,907	57,697	167/1032	62,708	1,437,354
2002	274,841	57,555	167/1034	67,000	1,547,669
2003	252,962	60,847	167/1093	70,642	1,661,996
2004	281,338	62,762	167/1127	71,022	1,618,987
2005	253,273	68,473	167/1127	73,243	1.702,562
2006	259,541	66,618	167/1123	66,860	1,112,542

awarded compensation to plaintiffs. Regardless of the size of the recreation or leisure service operation, self-insurance is a form of "Russian Roulette" that, if played long enough, will result in financial disaster. A solid risk management program can change the odds in favor of the provider.

There is little question that the insurance industry, the court system, and people who are willing to sue must equally share the blame for the present situation in which recreation service providers find themselves. Some reforms are needed within the insurance industry and within the legal system. Changes are very slow and normally require the strong voice (demand) of the U.S. public's attitude toward litigation (sometimes described as between greed and revenge) may take a long time to change from complacency to concern. In the meantime, it is essential to develop alternative methods to reduce the risk associated with providing recreation services. No one in the system is immune from litigation. Everyone from the custodian to the president of the board has some responsibility. Litigation is costly, frustrating, and time consuming.

Many facets of outdoor recreation feature risk as a vital and important element of the recreation experience. Mountain climbing, skydiving, skiing, scuba diving, whitewater rafting, theme park thrill rides, and many other recreation pursuits have elements of risk. Risk is the spice that makes some aspects of recreation so pleasurable and life itself more meaningful. *Life without risk is like life without life.* While the risk factors are very evident in many outdoor activities, they must also be manageable. Using sky diving as an example of high-risk recreation pursuit, it would be foolish and very risky not to place a great deal of importance on training, parachute rigging, and aircraft safety. A wise manager should also consider the use of waivers and releases in high-risk activities.

The standard by which a provider of recreation, both public and private, will be judged by the court is centered on reasonableness, sometimes referred to as the "reasonable man doctrine." That is, what would a reasonable man or woman do under the same circumstances? *It is the responsibility of an agency or organization to use ordinary and reasonable care to keep the premises reasonably safer for the visitor and to warn the visitor of any known danger.* Note the word "ordinary" in the above standard. A risk-management program allows us to work smarter and relax a little about the possibility of litigation. This book will increase a person's understanding of risk management and tort liability. It will also provide a practical approach to common risk management concerns.

Contents

1

What Are Torts? Why Do We Need to Understand What They Are?

KEYWORDS

Tort	*Plaintiff*	*CivilWrong*
Defendant	*Crime*	*Contract liability*
Negligence	*Personal liability*	*Strict liability*
Reasonable doubt	*Nuisance*	*Legal duty*
Intentional tort	*Federal and State torts*	*Constitutional tort*

The purpose of this chapter is to explain the difference between torts and crimes and to familiarize readers with a variety of legal terms.

Following this chapter you should be able to:

1. *Explain the difference between a civil wrong (tort) and a crime*
2. *Identify under what circumstances tort law governs the non-criminal relationships among people, business and governmental entities*
3. *Understand federal and state tort claims acts and recreation land-use statutes*
4. *Know why individuals and organizations could be held liable*
5. *Identify the negligence (civil) litigation process*

Legal scholars have been trying to define the word "tort" for more than a hundred years with the admission that a universally acceptable definition is yet to be found. "Tort" is derived from the Latin "tortum," which means twisted or distorted. *Webster's Dictionary* defines it as "a wrongful act, damage, or injury done willfully, negligently, or in circumstances involving strict liability, but not involving breach of contract, for which a civil suit can be brought."[4] *Black's Law Dictionary* defines tort, in part, as "a private or civil wrong or injury other than breach of contract, for which the court will provide a remedy in the form of an action for damages."[5] A tort consists of an action or lack of action, intentional or unintentional, that causes damages or property loss.

Example: A recreation provider who knows there is a structurally unsafe bridge on his property but allows people

A negligent act (caused by poor maintenance—a tort).

to use it could be subject to a civil suit (willful tort) if a person is injured as a result of the collapse of the bridge.

Example: An agency failed to properly maintain swings in a playground. A child was hurt when a support chain failed. The agency would be subject to a lawsuit (negligence tort) should there be a suit filed on behalf of the child.

Example: A municipal zoo has an animal cage that was constructed in a manner that allows the animal to bite visitors. The zoo would be subject to a suit (strict liability tort) if someone was bitten and an injury occurred.

If we add all the definitions and treatises together, it produces a vague image that a tort is a wrongful, non-criminal act that results in damage or injury to

A criminal act (damages could be awarded to the victim if suit is filed under civil law—a tort).

someone or something. The courts will determine how much a tort will cost the person who was legally liable.

THE DIFFERENCE BETWEEN A TORT (CIVIL WRONG) AND A CRIME

A crime is an offense against society, and penalties—usually jail sentences—are given for the "breach of public order." Civil law defines the rights of individuals in protecting themselves and their property against wrongful acts of another person.

In a criminal trial, the prosecution must prove the defendant guilty with a judgment standard of "beyond a reasonable doubt." In a civil trial, a *defendant*

(the party that is being accused of a wrong) and *plaintiff (the party that is complaining)* are on an equal footing because the judgment standard is based upon "the preponderance of evidence."

If a person is first convicted of a criminal offense, the fact that there was a prior criminal conviction (under the standard of "beyond a reasonable doubt") is enough evidence and carries enough weight to virtually guarantee a subsequent conviction in civil court. Therefore, when a party is injured as the result of a criminal act, the chances for successfully pursuing a civil judgment are significantly increased.

Example: A plaintiff is beaten severely by the defendant and the case is tried in a criminal court. If the jury finds the defendant guilty of criminal assault and battery, the plaintiff can then bring the case to civil court to force the defendant to pay for all the doctor bills and pain and suffering that resulted from the beating. The fact that the defendant was found guilty by a tougher standard (without a shadow of doubt) is usually enough evidence for the defendant to prevail in civil court.

If a plaintiff successfully pursues a suit in tort, they may receive compensation from the defendant for the wrongs done them. Four kinds of damages can be awarded by the courts as follows:

1. Consequential damages—Awarded to pay for the pain, suffering, injury, humiliation, and upset caused by the wrongdoing.[6]

2. Compensatory damages—Awarded to reimburse the plaintiff for any financial loss incurred as the result of the wrongdoing. This category includes special damages for such losses as medical, surgical, and hospital expenses and lost earnings.

3. Punitive or exemplary damages—Imposed when the wrong done is judged to have been inspired by malice or viciousness. They are intended to punish the wrongdoer.

As a point of common sense, it is simply not smart to sue someone in a civil court who does not have the means to pay the judgment of the court.

In addition to the above damages, attorney fees can also be awarded in special cases, such as suits brought for purposes of revenge or harassment, class action suits (suits brought by a number of plaintiffs related to the same issue) and civil rights, and employment rights litigation.

Tort law governs the non-criminal relationship among people, businesses, and governmental entities. It includes the following general categories:

Negligence (the main focus of this book)
1. Premises
2. Program Supervision
3. Facilities Supervision

Strict Liability
1. Animals
2. Product Liability
3. Food Service
4. Drinking Water
5. Dangerous Activities

Nuisance
1. User Injuries
2. Land Use
3. Controls

Intentional Torts
1. Personal
    a. Battery (unwanted touching)
    b. Assault (threats)
    c. False Imprisonment (confinement without arrest)
    d. Defamation (lies about one's character)
        i. Libel (written lies)
        ii. Slander (spoken lies)
2. Property
    a. Trespass to Land (going upon another's land without permission)
    b. Trespass to Chattels (property other than real estate)
    c. Conversion (dealing with property of another without right)

Constitutional Torts
1. Invasion of Privacy (right to be left alone)
2. Due Process (requirements of a search warrant, summons, hearings, etc. related to regulations and economic interests)
3. Liberty (right to freedom of movement)
4. Property (right to own property or be compensated for governmental taking)
5. Speech (right to say what one believes)
6. Religion (right to worship as one wishes)
7. Equal Protection (right of all citizens to be equally treated) regardless of:
    a. Race
    b. Ethnic Origin
    c. Gender
    d. Age
8. Civil Rights (rights guaranteed by constitution and other laws)

ELEMENTS OF TORT ACTIONS

The following three elements must be present before an act can be considered as a tort:

1. A breach of a legal duty that requires a person to conform to a certain standard to prevent injury or damages.
2. Some causal or direct connection between the legal duty and the resulting injury.
3. Actual loss or damage to the person or property of another.

CONTRACT LIABILITY

Contract liability is not covered specifically in this text; however, because of the numerous contracts recreation organizations engage in each year and the possibility of a suit evolving from a contract dispute or breach, a prudent administrator should consider the following in regard to proposed and existing contracts:

1. Authorization—Check with legal counsel to ascertain statutory authorization for the contract contemplated.
2. Contract Terms—Prior to entering into contract negotiations, the administrator should compile a list of nonnegotiable contract requirements. These requirements, along with compensation, contract time periods, and contract parties should be clearly identified. Contracts that are ambiguous and lack details are invitations to a breach and litigation. The administrator should be guided by the rule that the contract must be of sufficient detail to guarantee the level of service contemplated within a reasonable time period and for

adequate consideration. Unrealistic terms and criteria lead to problems. Incorporate all the agreed-to terms of the contract into the document. Verbal agreements that clarify or amplify a written contract will not be accepted as part of a contract. *It must be in writing.*

3. Bidding—Public agencies generally are required to seek bids on certain types of contracts or on contracts above certain dollar values. This procedure is governed by state statute as well as local procedures and ordinances. A prudent administrator should determine bid requirements and specifications prior to negotiating any contract.

Private organizations will also find that bidding reduces costs. Frequently, commercial recreation agencies, as a matter of corporate policy, seek bids on selected purchases. These procedures may not be as elaborate as the public bid process.

4. Contract Review—an administrator should develop policies and procedures for reviewing contracts with legal counsel. The key to successful contract reviews is in establishing and adhering to policy and procedure. Contract Law is a very complex area of the law, and the advice of legal counsel should be part of contract development. Attorneys should not make management and budget-related decisions on contracts, but should assist the administrator in preparing a contract document that is unambiguous and meets the goals sought by the parties.[7]

A federal negligence case is tried under the state laws where it occurred.

FEDERAL AND STATE TORT CLAIMS ACTS

The concept of sovereign immunity originated with the divine rights of kings; that is, "*The King can do no wrong.*" This concept carried over to governments at all levels in the United States because our legal system is based upon English Common Law. In our nation's early history we established a special court called the "Court of Claims" to hear tort claims against governmental entities. As the demand increased with our population, the special court proved to be awkward, expensive, and gave only limited accessibility to the general population.

In 1946, Congress passed the Federal Tort Claims Act (FTCA),[8] which makes the United States liable for torts that include the negligent or wrongful acts or omissions of federal employees or agencies. Federal liability is determined under the civil laws of the state where the wrong occurred. Parallel laws exist in the individual states that allow private citizens or organizations to sue state governments.

Example: A wrongful death resulted from a drowning accident that occurred on a beach managed by a federal land-managing agency. The civil case would be tried in a federal court in the state where the drowning occurred under the negligence laws of that state.

Some types of damages are excluded from claims under the FTCA in that the government shall "not be liable for . . . punitive damage."[9] The FTCA bars suits not begun within two years.[10] This limitation on time allowed to file a suit is commonly called a "statute of limitation." When the civil litigation is a state issue, recreation providers need to check with their local legal counsel to determine what the statutes of limitations are in their individual states.

The FTCA allows suits against agencies and their employees working within the scope of their employment in the same manner as private citizens are responsible for their acts.[11] When public employees are working within the scope of their employment they do not have to defend themselves; but rather, legal counsel for the jurisdiction involved will represent their interests in any litigation.[12]

One of the exceptions to the above rule provides that the government will not be liable for actions done with due care in the execution of a statute or regulation, even though it is invalid. This is referred to as the "discretionary function" of government. This allows public officials to perform duties such as budget and policy decisions within their discretionary function or duty without fear of suit.[13] The individual states have implemented state statutes that parallel the same concepts of the Federal Tort Claims Act. These state laws allow citizens to sue state agencies and employees for wrongful tort (negligent) acts.[14]

In all of the states, consent has been given to a greater or lesser extent to sue state and local agencies under tort. Usually permission to sue has been given to particular people under specific circumstances. In most cases the state statutes favor the state rather than the people of the state.[15] There is an excellent listing of the major elements of each state's Tort Claims Act and Government Sovereign Immunity in Betty van der Smissen's book entitled *Legal Liability and Risk Management for Public and Private Entities*.[16]

RECREATION LAND-USE STATUTES

The majority of states have enacted some form of Recreation Land-Use Liability Statutes.[17] Recreation-use liability statutes generally protect landowners, both public and private, from suit by non-fee-paying recreationists who use their property. As a general rule, the claimant must prove at least gross negligence[18] in order to establish a basis for pursuing a suit under the Recreation-Use Liability Statutes. Gross negligence is defined as an intentional failure to perform a duty in reckless disregard of the consequences. There is a higher level of negligence that exceeds gross negligence that is called "Willful and Wanton Negligence" that also negates the protection provided by the Recreation Land-Use Liability Statutes.

Example: A hunter enters onto state-owned-managed property to hunt deer. He falls into an erosion channel caused by a recent rainstorm and is severely injured. The state's Recreation Land-Use Liability Statute would shield the state from suit because the plaintiff did not pay a fee and would have to prove the state committed an act of "gross" negligence.

Under a recreational land-use liability statute, the landowner owes no duty to care for recreational users or to guard or warn against known or discoverable hazards on the premises. The protection from suit found under this statute is lost when a fee is charged for the use of the premises or the landowner is guilty of gross or willful and wanton misconduct. Unlike mere carelessness constituting negligence, willful/wanton misconduct is more outrageous behavior, demonstrating an utter disregard for the physical well-being of others. Willful and Wanton Negligence has a strong element of an intentional action by a defendant that

State recreation use liability statutes protect landowners.

When landowners require fees, recreation-use liability statutes do not apply.

is so obvious that he/she must be aware of it. It is usually accompanied by conscious indifference to the consequences, amounting almost to willingness.[19]

Example: The state's Recreational Land-Use Liability Statutes may not apply to a hunter who comes upon a farmer's property to hunt after paying the farmer a fee. When a fee is paid, the farmer must warn the hunter of known hazards and conduct safety inspections that would be normal for businesses. If the hunter has not paid a fee, the farmer owes the hunter no such warning.

It would be a prudent exercise for each outdoor recreation manager to carefully analyze his state's Recreation-Use Statutes. Some states have liability immunity statutes specifically written for their state-owned public lands.[20] At this time most of the Recreation-Use Liability Statutes apply to all public (local, county, state, and federal) and private lands within a state. Many state courts have been slow to determine if the recreation use liability statutes apply to government-managed lands.

Private and Quasi-Private Recreation Providers

Private corporations, such as racquetball or tennis clubs, or agencies such as the YMCA or Boy Scouts, are not governmental in nature and are not offered immunity from liability. However, because of their "public service" status, they are offered some limited immunity from liability. While an employee may have committed a negligent act, it may have been directed by policy or direction from above. The corporation, business, or agency may be liable for the negligent acts of its administrators, trustees, board, officers, and foreman as implementation of the "*doctrine of respondeat superior*" or "let the master answer."

The "*doctrine of respondeat superior*" has broad implications for the park, recreation, and leisure services field, for board and commissioner members, administrative officers, leaders, teachers, coaches, and volunteers. It means that employees and volunteers of public entities, as well as private corporations, normally cannot be held liable for their wrongful acts as long as they are performing within the scope of their assigned responsibilities.

The agency in which a person works is responsible for its employees' actions; however, this immunity does not apply if the person has violated criminal law or has not followed the rules and generally accepted standards of care.

Everyone in the work chain must know and act within the limits imposed by their job descriptions and their prescribed duties. As long as this is done, they will enjoy certain protection under the law. It is extremely important that everyone from board members—administrators, supervisors, employees, and volunteers—has a clear understanding of their duties and is properly trained.

Who is Liable?

If an accident due to personal negligence occurs, who is liable? You may be! If not you, your organization may be liable for damages. As a general rule, employees of agencies, volunteers, members of boards and commissions, and officers of private agencies, whether elected or appointed, are not personally liable for their actions as long as they are working within the scope of their duty. Supervisors and administrators could well be held personally liable in the following three circumstances:

1. If the administrator and/or supervisor participated in or in any way knowingly directed, ratified, or condoned the negligent act of an employee.

A recreation provider can be held liable for actions of an employee.

Example: If a park supervisor directed his or her employees to apply lawn chemicals that were known to be harmful to animals, and some household pets died or were made ill, the responsibility would be that of the supervisor.

2. Administrators and supervisors may be personally liable *for:*
   a. Incompetent hiring practices
   b. Failure to fire a person when circumstances warrant the dismissal
   c. Inadequate documentation of firing
   d. Inaccurate or incomplete job descriptions
   e. Insufficient training of staff
   f. Unclear establishment and/or enforcement of safety rules and regulations
   g. Failure to study and comply with statutory and/or corporation requirements
   h. Failure to remedy dangerous conditions
   i. Failure to give notice to others of known unsafe conditions

Example: An administrator of a recreation program hired a person to supervise a children's activity without first checking into whether the person had been arrested and convicted of any crime related to child molesting. If the new employee was subsequently involved in molesting a child, the administrator would be held negligent under civil law if the molestation took place in any way related to the program for which the person was hired.

An administrator can be held liable for poor hiring practices.

An administrator can be sued for discriminatory hiring practices.

3. Violations of a person's civil (Constitutional) rights.
   a. Religion, race, creed, color, gender, or age
   b. Rights of privacy
   c. Rights against illegal search and seizure
   d. Free speech
   e. Rights of assembly
   f. Freedom of association

Example: An administrator determined that he or she would not hire anyone over the age of 45 or a female, because the nature of the work was physically demanding. Such a policy could be subject to violations of a person's rights under the protected categories of the Civil Rights Bill and other federal legislation. It would be acceptable to have all people of all ages meet rigorous physical job requirements, but the application requirements cannot be related to unreasonable gender, age, or other protected categories limitations.

Because a person may not be personally liable does not diminish the fact that suits are exceptionally expensive, both in time and money to their organization or business—win or lose. It is very important that every individual in an organization recognizes personal responsibility to reduce the organization's exposure to negligence suits. If persons are named in a suit where they are indemnified (held harmless) by policy or statute, the legal counsel for that organization will represent them if necessary, and the damages will be paid by the organization or public agency. There are prescribed limits in most jurisdictions, usually statutory, as to what an organization is required to pay for recreation-related tort claims.

Special attention is paid to volunteers because recreation service agencies make extensive use of volunteers in a variety of roles. While their time and effort are not recognized with monetary rewards, each supervisor should consider them employees from a legal standpoint. Each volunteer working within the scope of his or her volunteer assignment subjects the organization to the same type of liability as do regular full-time employees. An injured volunteer can also sue the organization for any damages sustained due to a negligent act of another. It is important that all recreation administrators be extremely careful in recruiting, selecting, training, and supervising volunteers.

Example: A park manager uses volunteers to conduct interpretive programs on the property. One of the approved volunteers strikes out and hits a visitor who has said something distasteful to her. The park would be subject to suit over the incident just as if the volunteer were a full-time employee of the park.

Effective risk-management programs will examine the property, facilities, policies, contracting, and the supervision aspects of recreation services.

THE LITIGATION (CIVIL) PROCESS

In order for individuals and organizations to understand what type of evidence and what is involved in the litigation process, they need to know the following sequence of events that will take place:

Pre-Trial Phase Sequence

1. An incident occurs causing an injury or property loss
2. A complaint or summons is filed, requested by the plaintiff and issued by the court
3. Defendant answers the complaint within a strict time allowance

4. Motions are made by both the defendant and plaintiff for a default judgment (if the answer was not timely), dismissal, summary judgment, etc.
5. If the trial moves forward, the discovery period starts and includes investigation, depositions, interrogatories, and production of documents
6. Pre-trial conference is held before the judge in an effort to negotiate a settlement

Trial Phase Sequence

1. Jury selection
2. Opening statement by plaintiff and defendant (plaintiff goes first)
3. Presentation of plaintiff's case (cross examination by the defendant's witnesses)
4. Presentation of defendant's case (cross examination by the plaintiff's witnesses)
5. Closing arguments by plaintiff and defendant
6. Instructions by the judge if there is a sitting jury
7. Verdict by the judge or jury
8. Sometimes judge issues a judgment that counters a civil jury's verdict. It is called "Judgment Notwithstanding Verdict (JNV)."
9. If appropriate, motions are made for appeal of verdict based upon abuse of discretion, findings of fact, and mistakes (errors).

An administrator can be held liable for the actions of a recognized volunteer.

NEGLIGENCE (CIVIL) LITIGATION PROCESS

PRE-TRIAL PHRASE

Incident–Injury or Property Loss

↓

Complaint or Summons–Requested by Plaintiff and Issued by Court

↓

Answer to Complaint–Defendant

↓

Motions for Default Judgment, Dismissal, Summary Judgment, etc.

↓

Discovery–Depositions, Interrogatories, and Production of Documents

↓

Pre-Trial Conference–An Effort for Negotiated Settlement

↓

Trial Phrase

Jury Selection

↓

Opening Statements by Plaintiff and Defendant

↓

Presentation of Plaintiff's Case (Cross Examination by Defense)

↓

Presentation of Defense's Case (Cross Examination by Plaintiff)

↓

Closing Arguments by Plaintiff and Defendant

↓

Instructions by the Judge–In Jury Trials

↓

Jury (or Judge) Verdict

↓

Judgment or Judgment Notwithstanding Verdict

↓

Appeal Verdict Based on Abuse of Discretion, Findings of Fact, and Mistakes

Chapter

2

Negligence

KEYWORDS

Negligence

Res ispa loquitur (the thing speaks for itself)

Reasonable man doctrine

Punitive damages

Misfeasance

Assumption of risk

Gross negligence

Failure of proof

Foreseeability

Waivers, releases, agreements to participate

Proximate cause

Breach of duty

Compensatory damages

Nonfeasance

Joint tort-feasor

Ordinary negligence

Governmental immunity

Rule of seven

Statute of limitations

Legal duty

Injury and damages

Standard of care

Consequential damages

Malfeasance

Comparative negligence

Willful or wanton negligence

Notice of claims

Statute of limitations

The purpose of this chapter is to explore the elements of negligent behavior and the ramifications of such actions. Following this chapter you should be able to:

1. Know the four elements critical to understanding negligence

2. Be aware of the various degrees of negligent behavior

3. Know what defense mechanisms are available to you in negligence cases

4. Identify what laws pertain to your state in comparative negligent claims

5. Understand governmental immunity

6. Know the basic principles behind waivers, releases and agreements to participate

Negligence has been defined as a lack of due diligence or care; however, from a legal perspective negligence could also be the act of doing something that should not have been done.[21] *Black's Law Dictionary* defines negligence as "The omission to do something which a reasonable man, guided by those ordinary considerations . . . would do, or the doing of something which a reasonable and prudent man would not do."[22]

ELEMENTS OF NEGLIGENCE

Whether negligence exists depends upon the particular circumstances related to each case. The laws and court decisions are very complex and will decide

A recreation provider may not be held liable because of unsafe actions of others.

who is at fault, so few generalities can be applied. Certain elements must be proved in order to have a viable negligence court case. They include:

1. It must be proved that the defendant has a legal duty of care; that is to be legally responsible to the plaintiff.
2. The plaintiff must prove there was either a failure to perform a required task or a breach of duty.
3. There must be some direct connection between the damages and the actions or lack of actions by the defendant. Simply stated, the plaintiff must prove that the breach of duty is the cause of the injury. This is commonly called "proximate cause."
4. A plaintiff must prove that he suffered damages, i.e., a physical injury, mental anguish, or financial loss.

THE LEGAL DUTY (FIRST ELEMENT)

Whether or not there is a legal duty in negligence cases is a question of law. It is something that is determined by the judge, not the jury. The court decides whether the level of conduct was sufficient to prove unreasonable risk. It should be noted that the entire field of recreation has an element of risk. Risk can also be described as danger, hazard, or loss, that is the result of an adventure, thrills, and physical exertion.[23]

Example: A child on a park swing is exposed to a certain amount of risk. The sponsor of the playground provides the equipment, surfacing, layout, and design that meet all the recommended guidelines of the American Society for Testing and Materials (ASTM) and the U.S. Consumers Product Safety Commission (USCPSC). The sponsor cannot guarantee that a child will not get hurt falling out of the swing or because of the unsafe act of another child. An unreasonable risk occurs when the sponsor fails to conform to the accepted guidelines and creates an unsafe playground. Unreasonable risk occurs when the conduct falls below acceptable guidelines and normal safety practices.

Reasonable Man Doctrine

The reasonable man doctrine or standard of care compares the actions of an individual with that of a reasonable man in the same or similar circumstances. The conduct of this hypothetical, prudent, and careful person will vary somewhat and likely combine both objective and subjective elements, including physical attributes, mental capacity, and special skills.

Regarding physical attributes—the reasonable person should possess those characteristics typical of his or her circumstances. If, by chance, the person is mute, blind, or deaf or otherwise disabled, he or she must act as a reasonable person with the same circumstances. Such persons are entitled to live in the world and to have allowances made for their disabilities.

Managers must make "allowances" for the type of visitors they may reasonably expect. As an example, if a recreation area attracts very young children, rather than place warning signs that a child cannot read near a hazardous condition, the prudent manager would place a physical barrier between the young visitor and the potential danger (i.e., a fence).

A wise recreation manager will have a sign stating PARENT/CHILD PLAYGROUND rather than PLAYGROUND. The distinct difference in the signing should be that the parents understand that they are part of the playground experience—they are there to provide supervision, limit the activities, and make risk decisions for the child. International signs or bilingual signs may be necessary in some environments. In American culture, all too many parents drop their young children off at the playground rather than play with their children in the playground. Children's playgrounds should have equipment designed to facilitate both parent and child usage.

When considering mental capacity, there is no allowance made for minor mental deficiencies. Defendants will be held to the test of reasonable conduct in the same manner as the prudent and careful person. Yet, if that "mental capacity" is a reflection of young minds (immaturity) that are unable to comprehend danger or respond to written warning, special attention must be given to the situation.

Park, recreation, and leisure professionals who work with and service diverse populations are required to exercise reasonable care in what they do, but also

Recreation providers should not take upon themselves the supervision of others when it is not necessary.

need to possess a certain amount of technical knowledge on the activities they supervise.

An outdoor recreation manager may have a high-risk activity on the property he/she manages, i.e., skate park. The question that should be asked is, "What type of skills, equipment, and facility design are needed to reduce the risk of the activity?" A certification system should be used to determine the competency of the high-risk user. Certain high-risk recreation activity leaders need a minimum amount of training under a certified instructor, specialized equipment, and more than one participant (a buddy system) prior to engaging in an activity. Some high-risk activities needing "certification" may include spelunking, mountain climbing, whitewater canoeing, hunting, wilderness use, and many other activities. Waivers, releases, and agreements to participate may be effective tools to reduce litigation for adults engaged in high-risk activities.

Volunteers and part-time employees are held to the same standard of care as full-time employees. A discerning manager will never place them in the position of taking responsibilities for the safety, training, or general well-being of all the visitors, particularly young people.

Example: Mrs. Jones brought her fifth grade class to a park for an environmental education field trip. Mrs. Jones

wants to take a coffee break and requests that the interpreter "take charge" while she goes on her break. She should always be required to accompany the class. Her request to take a coffee break should be refused. Mrs. Jones' continued presence and supervision of the class provides an important barrier between the agency (park) and possible legal action should an accident occur involving one of the students. The agency's responsibility is that of providing environmental training, not supervision.

Rule of Seven
(Comparative Liability Doctrine)

The care expected of children is not the same as that expected of adults. The courts recognize that society is very protective of youth. The level of care depends on the age of the child. Children are held in various degrees of responsibility for their own actions. This is sometimes referred to as the "Rule of Seven." The four general age categories are as follows:

1. Essentially, children under the age of seven (seven or under years of age) are not responsible for their own welfare. A child under seven normally cannot recognize dangerous situations or read warning signs. Our greatest responsibility for supervision lies with this age group.
2. Children between seven and fourteen (seven to 14 years of age) are considered partially responsible for their own welfare. They can understand most warning signs and can comprehend some dangerous situations.
3. Youth fourteen through legal adulthood (18-21 years of age) are mostly responsible for their own actions. They have the experience to make many good decisions related to their personal danger.
4. Adults are considered responsible for their behavior.

In some courts the "Rule of Seven" is not a recognized legal doctrine; however, the principles and concepts still apply as is relates to comparative negligent doctrine. It is important to note that the courts have modified the application of the "Seven Rule" when circumstances warranted modification, such a mental limitation, or other factors.

Foreseeability

Like many aspects of law, certain doctrines are very difficult to understand. There are many interpretations and opinions on what is foreseeable and what is not foreseeable. The ability of a person to foresee a danger depends on the individual's training and experience. Foreseeability is the ability to see or know in advance there is a reasonable anticipation that harm or injury may result because of certain acts or omissions. "As a necessary element of proximate cause this means that the wrongdoer is not responsible for consequences which are merely possible, but is responsible only for consequences which are probable according to ordinary and usual experience."[24] Perhaps a simpler way of stating it would be to say the courts do not demand that the manager possess "mind-reading" skill, but they do expect reasonable anticipation of risk and common sense. Whether or not a legal duty exists is a question of law to be determined by the court. Once the duty has been established by the court, it is the jury's or judge's responsibility to determine if the defendant conformed to a standard of care of reasonable prudence and foresight sufficient to protect the plaintiff against unreasonable risk.

BREACH OF DUTY (SECOND ELEMENT)

Once a standard of care is established, the second element of negligence comes into play—that of failure to conform to the duty. Negligent conduct may occur because a person did something that was dangerous, or the same negligent conduct could occur because a person failed to do something. What is important from a liability standpoint is that a defendant was somehow involved in the activity that resulted in an accident.[25]

There are three words that describe the type of breach involved with a negligent act by a public official: nonfeasance, misfeasance, and malfeasance. They can be very important in determining the severity of the breach of duty and therefore the liability of the defendant(s).[26] *Black's Law Dictionary* describes the differences in the types of negligent acts as follows:[27]

***Res Ipsa Loquitur*—the action speaks for itself.**

1. *Nonfeasance*—Nonperformance of some act which ought to be performed, omission to perform a required duty at all, or total neglect of duty.
2. *Misfeasance*—The improper performance of some act which a man may lawfully do.
3. *Malfeasance*—Evil doing; ill conduct, the commission of some act which is positively unlawful.

Res Ipsa Loquitur

There are certain legal phrases that have no short, easily understood substitute words. "*Res ipsa loquitur*" is one of those phrases. The literal Latin translation is, "The thing speaks for itself." The phrase represents a rule of evidence whereby the negligence of the alleged wrongdoer may be inferred from the mere factual circumstances of the accident. To apply this doctrine two things must happen:

1. The accident or damage would not have occurred if reasonable care had been used.
2. All the elements of the circumstances surrounding the accident were under the control of the defendant.

The doctrine can be further exhibited when there is no direct evidence to show cause of injury

Proximate cause—the accident must have been caused by an act or omission of the defendant.

A person may blame anyone, but the court will determine the actual cause.

and the detailed circumstantial evidence indicates that the negligence of the defendant is the most plausible explanation for the injury.[28]

Example: If a person backs his/her automobile into another automobile in a parking garage, there is little doubt about who caused the accident . . . the act speaks for itself. That is res ipsa loquitur.

Most United States courts regard *res ipsa loquitur* as nothing more than one form of circumstantial evidence.[29] State courts are more likely to apply the principles of *res ipsa loquitur*.

Proximate Cause (Third Element)

In order to prove negligence the plaintiff must prove that there was a relationship between the plaintiff's accident or damage and the negligent act or lack of what should have been done by the defendant.

Example: When parents make a claim of injury on behalf of their child as a result of an injury on a playground, the plaintiff's parents must prove that the accident occurred on the defendant's playground as the result of the defendant's negligence.

Proximate cause is not a simple element, but is rather a very complex problem made up of a number of different circumstances, which are not distinguished clearly by the law. A defendant can always point to someone or something else as the "actual" cause of the accident. As a legal matter, legal responsibility for the cause of an accident must be limited to those causes which are closely connected with the result. They must be connected with such significance that the law is justified in imposing liability.[30]

Example: If a person has an automobile accident, he/she can always blame his/her parents, the driving instructor, or the maker of the automobile. The Biblical "Adam and Eve" or "the devil made me do it" could well be the ultimate responsible persons or proximate cause of the accident. The courts determine the proximate cause in a reasonable manner. Normally, the driver will be the proximate cause of the accident.

Injury and Damages (Fourth Element)

There must be actual loss or damage to the interests of another. There can be no negligence without injury to person or property loss.

The word "damage" refers to loss, injury, or deterioration caused by negligence. Damage can involve physical harm, mental harm, or damage to property. Damages awarded can include any or all of the categories of compensatory, punitive, or consequential. The three categories of damages are described as follows:[31]

1. *Compensatory Damages*—Damages awarded to a person as compensation, indemnity, or restitution for harm sustained.
2. *Punitive Damages*—Damages awarded to a person to punish the other litigants because of their outrageous conduct.
3. *Consequential Damages*—Damages awarded a person for suffering because of the act of another even though the act was not directed toward the first person specifically and the damages did not occur immediately.[32]

DEGREE OF NEGLIGENCE

The words "simple," "ordinary," "gross," "willful," "wanton," and "reckless" are used to modify the degree of negligence in most courts. Some believe there are no "degrees" of negligence, only different amounts of care required. Whatever legal position prevails matters little. The important consideration is that a negligent act will be judged by the defendant's intent. For purposes of defining the degree of negligence, the following are the most commonly used:

1. *Ordinary Negligence*—The failure to exercise such care as would be expected by the majority of people under like circumstances.[33]
2. *Gross Negligence*—The disregard of life and property of others. This exhibits as very great negligence or as the want of even slight care. It consists of conscious acts of negligence.[34]
3. *Willful or Wanton Negligence*—The conduct complained of was so "gross" as to have something of a criminal character, or be deemed equivalent to an evil intent, wantonness, or recklessness indicative of malice.[35]

JOINT TORT-FEASOR

A tortfeasor is someone who commits a tort. Negligence can be shared by two or more defendants. This is usually referred to as "joint tort-feasor." In the case of joint tortfeasor the damages would be assigned to the individual defendants by the judge. The "deep pocket" doctrine applies; that is, those who have the financial means will be assigned all or most of the damages by the court if one or more of the co-defendants are not financially able to bare the burden of the court's judgment.

A number of people may be named as co-defendants.

Example: If a child is hurt on a playground swing, the plaintiff will likely name the park sponsor, the maintenance manager, the employees responsible for the equipment, the director of the managing public agency, the contractor who installed the equipment, and the company that manufactured the equipment as joint tort-feasor.

DEFENSES IN NEGLIGENCE

An overview of the defenses in negligence will allow you to understand the viability of claims against you or your agency. The major defenses are:

1. Assumption of Risk
2. Comparative Negligence
3. Contributory Negligence
4. Governmental Immunity

5. Failure of Proof
6. Notice of Claim
7. Statute of Limitations
8. Release or Waiver or Agreement to Participate

Assumption of Risk

A person may not recover from injuries received when they voluntarily subjected themselves to a known and appreciated danger. Requirements are that:[36]

1. The plaintiff has knowledge that the activity engaged in has dangerous elements.
2. The plaintiff appreciates the nature and extent of the danger.
3. The plaintiff subjects self to the danger.

Participants in recreation and sports cannot assume risk for something when they do not know the inherent danger of the activity, do not comprehend the risk in relation to their physical and mental capabilities, or do not appreciate the magnitude of possible injury. Participants only assume the risk for aspects inherent in the activity. They may properly assume that it is the duty of the sponsoring agency to provide appropriate and safe facilities, equipment, instruction, and supervision. Young children, to some degree, do not appreciate the nature and extent of dangerous situations. Defendants cannot use the assumption of risk defense effectively to block suits brought by children or their parents.

Example: If people choose to engage in whitewater canoeing, they assume a risk that the canoe may turn over with resulting injuries or even death. However, if the outfitter that furnishes the canoeing equipment provides canoes that are known to be particularly dangerous or unsafe, then the outfitter may be negligent. If the provider fails to warn the canoeist of dangerous high water, then the assumption of risk defense may not be applicable.

Comparative Negligence

In States that have comparative negligence laws, plaintiffs can recover even if they contributed significantly to their own accident. Most of the states have some form of law that allows recovery when part of the fault belongs with the plaintiff. Comparative negligence laws place upon either the defendant or the plaintiff the entire burden of the loss for which both the defendant and plaintiff are, in fact, responsible to some degree.[37] It is important to understand the four main classifications of comparative negligence as follows:[38]

1. *Pure Comparative Negligence*—Allows the plaintiff to sue regardless of level of his or her own contribution to the injury or damage, unless the plaintiff is 100 percent at fault.

Example: If a plaintiff skier, under pure comparative negligence law, was 80 percent at fault and the defendant was 20 percent at fault and the plaintiff's damages were $10,000, the plaintiff would receive $2,000.

2. *Fifty-Percent (50%) Rule*—Bars recovery if the plaintiff's negligence is greater than that of the defendant.

Example: Under the Fifty-Percent Rule, if a plaintiff was 51% or more at fault and the defendant was 49 percent or less at fault, the plaintiff would not be able to recover any damages. If fault was determined 51 percent for the defendant and 49 percent for the plaintiff, the plaintiff would receive 51 percent of the damages awarded by the court.

Participants assume some risks for known dangerous activities, but they are not responsible for defective equipment.

3. *Forty-nine Percent (49%) Rule*—Bars recovery unless the plaintiff's negligence is less than that of the defendant.

Example: Under the Forty-nine Percent Rule, if a plaintiff was 50 percent at fault and the defendant was 50 percent at fault, the plaintiff would not be able to recover. The defendant must be at least 51 percent at fault for the plaintiff to recover.

Comparative negligence is an important fact determining liability.

4. *Slight/Gross Rule*—Bars recovery unless the plaintiff's negligence was slight and the defendant's negligence was gross by comparison.[39]

Example: If the plaintiff contributes any more than a slight amount of negligence to an accident, the plaintiff cannot recover.

The following is a summary of comparative negligence laws by States:

COMPARATIVE NEGLIGENCE LAWS BY STATE

States with Pure Comparative Negligence:

Alaska, Arizona, California, Florida, Illinois, Louisiana, Iowa, Kentucky, Michigan, Missouri, Mississippi, New Mexico, New York, Rhode Island, Washington, and Puerto Rico.

States with Fifty-Percent (50%) Rule:

Connecticut, Delaware, Hawaii, Indiana, Massachusetts, Minnesota, Montana, Nevada, New Hampshire, New Jersey, Ohio, Oklahoma, Oregon, Pennsylvania, Texas, Vermont, Wisconsin, and the Virgin Islands.

States with Forty-nine (49%) Rule:

Arkansas, Colorado, Georgia, Idaho, Kansas, Maine, North Dakota, Utah, West Virginia, and Wyoming

States with Slight-Gross Rule:

Nebraska, South Dakota, and Tennessee

States Without Comparative Negligence Principles*:

Alaska, Alabama, Maryland, North Carolina, South Carolina, and Virginia

* These states have some judicial adoption of the principle, but the principle is interpreted on the case-by-case basis.

Contributory Negligence

The term "contributory negligence" is basically outdated by the principles of comparative negligence; however, it still remains an important factor in considering a defense of a negligence action. The contributory negligence defense is invoked when a plaintiff contributes to his/her injury or damage to such an extent that they, the plaintiff, breached an expected standard of conduct. In most states (see chart above), the doctrine of contributory negligence has been replaced by comparative negligence rules.[40]

Example: A plaintiff is injured in an off-road vehicle accident on a mountain trail. She alleges that the managing agency allowed the trail to be used after they had knowledge that the trail was severely eroded. An investigation of the incident found that the plaintiff had in fact left the trail as a result of traveling at a excessive speed. The plaintiff contributed so significantly to her accident that a court action could not be brought against the agency.

Although somewhat outdated, there is an "act of God" defense that has been placed under this category for simplicity purposes. Some jurisdictions consider "Acts of God" to be an extension of the principles of contributory negligence. These are usually referred to as conditions caused by the natural elements.[41]

Example: A plaintiff was sailing on an inland lake when a sudden wind tipped the rented boat and caused injury to the plaintiff and damage to the boat. The courts would not allow legal action to be pursued because the wind was a natural element. The lake-managing agency and the boat rental company are not required to provide warning for natural elements they would be unable to predict, i.e., earthquakes, sudden weather changes, or lightning, etc.

If a person contributes significantly to his own accident, he is barred from suing.

Some accidents are caused by "Acts of God." Suits are barred under these circumstances.

The most common change of the rule of contributory negligence is the doctrine of the "Last Clear Chance." If a defendant or plaintiff has the last clear chance to avoid an injury or damage, then the other's negligent act is not the proximate cause of the accident.[42] In order to understand this doctrine, emphasis should be placed on the word "clear" so that everyone understands there is no doubt about the accident being avoidable.

Example: A man engaged in cross-country skiing came upon a sign that read "Danger—Do Not Enter—Avalanche Area." He skied around the sign and became entrapped and died in an avalanche. The man's family sued the managing agency personnel for the loss of his life because they failed to stop him from entering the dangerous area. The court would rule that the deceased man had the last clear chance to avoid the accident and would disallow the suit.

Governmental Immunity

In the federal and state government the doctrine of "Sovereign Immunity" or "The King Can Do No Wrong" has been abolished. Governmental immunity is limited in scope, but continues as a viable defense in some categories of damages. Most states have laws that limit the amount of claims or eliminates claims in certain categories of administration, usually referred to as discretionary functions. As examples, the govern-

If a plaintiff had a "last clear chance" to avoid the accident, he is barred from suing.

Planning and policy decisions are not subject to suit because of government immunity.

ment is usually immune from suits regarding personnel actions, budget distribution, decisions involving the planning and policy levels, legislative actions, and administrative processes. These categories are generally not subject to litigation and are considered discretionary in the courts.[43]

Example: A park visitor is upset and attempts to sue the government because an agency did not allocate enough money to properly take care of a recreation site. The visitor would not be able to sue because of the immunity afforded the budgeting aspect of government.

Failure of Proof

All four of the elements of negligence (duty, breach of duty, proximate cause, and damages) must be proved before negligence can be found. The plaintiff has the burden to prove each of the four elements. Failure to prove will result in dismissal in the pre-pleading stage of litigation.

Example: If a woman can prove that a park agency had a duty to keep the sidewalks safe, that there was an unsafe crack in the sidewalk, and that this sidewalk crack caused the person to fall, the plaintiff will still be unable to prove negligence unless the woman can prove that the resultant accident did, in fact, cause injury or damages.

Notice of Claim

The federal government, most state statutes, and many municipal ordinances require an injured or damaged person to file a notice of claim within a certain time period, usually 30 to 120 days.[44]

The notice of claim allows the agency to conduct an investigation into the validity of each claim and settle the legitimate claims. Some courts debate whether failure to provide a notice is a valid reason for denying the opportunity of an individual to make legal claim

A plaintiff must prove the agency had a duty, the duty was breached, the breach was the proximate cause, and damages occurred.

against governmental agencies. Claim notices should include a minimum of the following items about the accident or damage:[45]

MINIMUM INFORMATION ON NOTICE OF CLAIM

1. Dates
   a. Date of accident
   b. Date of claim
2. Time of accident
3. Location of accident
4. Type of injury or damage
5. Witness(es) to accident
6. How accident occurred
7. Amount of damages (actual bills or estimates)[45]

In most jurisdictions a claim must be made within a specific time period before a suit is allowed.

Example: If a man is injured in a swimming beach and feels the accident occurred as the result of poor maintenance of the facility, he must submit a claim for his injury to the managing agency or organization. The governmental agency with responsibility for the beach must then determine through investigation the legitimacy of the claim. If the claimant feels he was not compensated for the injury, he can refuse the offer and file a suit in civil court. If he failed to file a claim against the organization or agency they may not likely be allowed to sue.

A young person (minor) normally has until the time he or she reaches majority to file a claim. A person that is incapacitated due to illness or some other legitimate reason, can rightfully wait to file a claim until they gain the mental or physical capability to proceed with the filing.

Statute of Limitations

States have varying amounts of time allowed between the time of an accident and when a suit must be filed. The statutes that govern this time period are called "Statutes of Limitations." For simple negligence cases, that time period averages about two to three years; however, some states have variations of those time periods. Certain categories of claims, such as property damage, may have longer statutes

of limitations than do personal injuries, wrongful death, or libel.

Example: If a man were injured in an accident in the state of Indiana on July 1, 2004, and attempted to file a suit on August 12, 2006, he would not have been able to sue. Indiana has a two-year statute of limitation, and the time period between the accident and the filing exceeded two years.

A child can wait until he or she has reached majority before filing a suit. The parents may sue on behalf of the child prior to the child reaching the age of majority. If the suit is pursued by the parents, the child may not file an additional suit after he/she reaches the age of majority.

Waivers, Releases, and Agreements to Participate

Waivers, releases, and agreements to participate are not normally considered a part of tort doctrine, but rather are documents that tends to justify, excuse, or clear the defendant from fault or guilt raising from an accident or damages.[46] These documents must be written to be effective. Verbal waivers are too challengeable to be effective. Waivers and releases are contracts. The court's response to waivers and releases

A suit must be filed within a specific time period established by state law.

has varied with individual judges and jurisdictions. Since minors are unable to contract, the use of waivers and releases to waive the rights to use would be considered improper.

RELEASES, WAIVERS AND AGREEMENTS TO PARTICIPATE ARE INVALID IF THEY ARE:

1. Signed by minors (children and youth under legal age of majority).
2. Signed on behalf of minors by their parents or guardians. Adults cannot sign away the legal rights of their children.
3. The release or waiver is not specific. Ambiguity in the content of the waiver makes it difficult to determine the extent of the rights waived.
4. Waiving rights contrary to public policy.[47]

Example: A 16-year-old youth signs a waiver that states they will not file suit against a public park agency if an accident occurs during the periods of transportation or at the recreation activity. The bus is involved in a vehicle accident, injuring the youth. It is determined that the bus driver was legally drunk at the time of the accident. The waiver would be invalid for any one of three reasons:

1. *The waiver was not specific.*
2. *The waiver was signed by the minor.*
3. *The act of driving while drinking is against public policy and therefore rights cannot be waived.*

It should be noted that waivers and releases have a higher likelihood of being validated by the courts if they are specific and are related to high-risk activities such as whitewater rafting, mountain climbing, spelunking, etc.

With all the criticism and limitations placed upon waivers and releases, recreation providers should still not be hesitant to use them with their adult participants. When they are specific they provide the participant with a strong reminder as to the dangers involved with the activity. That reminder, accompanied by a signature, forms a basis whereby the participant cannot deny that he did not know the dangers involved; thereby a specific waiver, release, or agreement to participate invokes the "assumption of risk" defense.

The best legal instrument to limit the liability for minors is the "agreement to participate." This document must be specifically worded to cover the risks and dangers involved in the activity in detail. It also must include the rules of participant conduct and equipment and clothing requirements for safety and organization purposes so the minors and their parents/guardians understand what is expected of them. The *Agreement to Participate* document that the parents

A waiver or release must be specific, not signed by a minor, or allow a practice that is against public policy.

have reviewed and understand the dangers involved and have allowed their minor children to participate in the activity and agree to inform their children in the rules and safety aspects of their activity.[48] The agreement to participate places the decision making on the parents rather than the child.

An effective *Agreement to Participate* document triggers the assumption of risk theory defense to negligence. In order for the assumption of risk defense to hold in court, the risks involved in the activities must be thoroughly described.

It should be obvious from the above principles that there is much less risk providing recreation activities for adult participants compared to serving youth participants. That is fact. However, public recreation agencies have an obligation, in an ethical sense, if not a legal responsibility, to serve that segment of the population that is most vulnerable to accidents and that needs to be protected from harm . . . youth.

Chapter

3

Standard of Care

Key Words

Standard of care

Trespasser

Invitee

Licensee

Self-incrimination

Recreation use statutes

Reasonable prudent person

Attractive nuisance

The purpose of this chapter is to explain the standard of care each agency must provide its users.
Following this chapter you should be able to:

1. *Identify the basic standard of care required of a reasonable prudent person working for your agency*
2. *Know how to determine a person's status as an invitee, licensee, or trespasser*
3. *Learn what an attractive nuisance is*

Every recreation provider has a "standard of care" they owe the people who use their services, drink their water, go upon their property, eat their food, or use their equipment. Standard of care is defined as that degree of care which a reasonably prudent person should exercise under same or similar circumstances.[49] If a recreation provider fails to provide for customers in a "reasonably prudent" manner and that failure results in damages, the recreation provider may be liable for the damages caused.

A jury in a negligence case will be given instructions by the judge to determine if the defendant met the standard of care established by the law. In the absence of statutes to establish a standard, the jury will be instructed to determine whether the defendant met the standard of an ordinary and prudent person . . . something that is a standard practice for that activity or service. In the pre-trial phase of the litigation, the defendant recreation provider will be asked to provide any agency or organization manuals and handbooks that are related to the case. This is called "discovery" (see p. 9) and is a component of the evidence-gathering process. It is important that recreation providers have internal manuals and handbooks that meet

Agencies and organizations must meet the "standard of care" established for the activity or facility.

national and local standards of care. Some caution is necessary to make certain that manual and handbook requirements are not superfluous or that written or assigned high standards of performance that cannot be met because of manpower or budgetary limitations. Excessive standards need to be modified so the documents will not become "self-incriminating" during the legal process.

Example: A recreation agency (defendant) is sued as a ... storm and injuring ... "God" ... flaws ... agency ... ections of ... ed inspection rate of one per year). The age... produce any records that indicate the trees have been chec... for soundness during the past three years. The recreation agency had two major problems that will jeopardize its case:

A recreation provider owes different standards of care to users, depending whether they are invitees, permittees, or trespassers.

1. Not meeting its own standards.

2. Not documenting the inspection it conducted.

The determination of a person's status is a critical element in deciding what standard of care must be provided. This determination is also a very complex issue that varies from state to state. Some states no longer have status classifications; however, the general principles still apply. In general, persons who visit park, recreation, and leisure facilities, whether public or private, are classified as invitees, licensees, or trespassers or they are in a special category of visitor. The duty owed by the recreation provider to each of these categories can and does vary. The recreation provider owes the invitee the highest duty of care, the licensee a duty to warn of known dangers, and the trespasser the least warning and protection.

Example: A park manager has three persons on her property: one who has paid a fee and entered to use the park (an invitee), one who is there to service the soda machine (a licensee), and one who is there because he crawled under the fence to use the park without paying a fee (a trespasser). The park manager would owe a different standard of care to each of the above users.

INVITEE

An invitee is one who is at a place at the invitation of another and usually has compensated the recreation provider for services or use of the facilities. It is further described as follows:[50]

An invitee is either a public invitee or a business invitee. The following defines the two categories of invitees:

1. A public invitee is a person who is invited to enter or remain on land as a member of the public for a purpose for which the land is held open to the public.
2. A business invitee is a person who is invited to enter or remain on land for a purpose directly or indirectly connected with the business dealing with the possessor of the land.

In the case of invitees, the owner, operators, and managers have a duty to assure that reasonable care has been used to prepare the premises and make them safe for the visitors. This includes protection from injury related to condition of the land, facilities, or equipment or by injury from third parties. In the case of invitees, the owner, operator, or manager must inspect the premises, remove or warn of potential hazards, and as a general rule exercise reasonable care to protect users. Kaiser describes the duties a recreation provider or landowner owes the invitee as follows:[51]

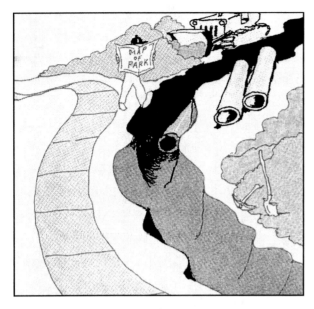

Agencies and organizations should foresee hazards and protect visitors from them.

People who enter upon a recreation provider's property for service or business purposes are owed reasonable care.

DUTIES OF RECREATION PROVIDERS FOR INVITEES

1. Keep the premises in safe repair.
2. Inspect the premises to discover hidden hazards.
3. Remove the known hazards or warn of their presence.
4. Anticipate foreseeable uses and activities by invitees and take reasonable precautions to protect invitees from foreseeable dangers.
5. Conduct operations on the premises with reasonable care for the safety of the invitee.

The prudent operator who complies with these five steps and keeps a written and dated record of periodic inspection and repairs will be able to mount an impressive defense against potential legal actions.

Example: A recreation provider would be subject to a negligence suit if an invitee was injured as a result of a fall into a construction trench adjacent to a walkway. The court would likely determine that the recreation provider should have foreseen the possibility of someone falling into the trench. The recreation provider should have constructed a barrier and/or warned of the danger.

LICENSEE

The "licensee" classification of user is owed a duty of care by the recreation provider that falls in the moderate category. There are no distinct dividing lines among the three categories, and a great deal of "gray" area exists among the various classifications. The licensee is basically someone who has the permission or consent, expressed or implied, to go on the land for his or her own purpose.[52] In most jurisdictions the recreation provider owes the licensee the duty of reasonable or due care.[53] The licensee may go upon the recreation provider's land to conduct business or to the mutual advantage of both the licensee and the owner or occupant.[54] A licensee's stay on the land is usually short in duration. Licensees need to be warned of any known dangers on the property.

Example: A postal carrier enters upon the land of a recreation provider to deliver mail and is injured in a fall that resulted from black ice (hard-to-see ice) on a sidewalk. The carrier is a licensee with implied consent to enter upon the property without specific permission. The landowner should anticipate the use of the land by many types of licensees, i.e., postal personnel, gas and electric meter readers, contractors, business associates, etc. The landowner should have warned the postal carrier of non-obvious condition by sign or some other means.

There is a distinction made between a licensee, whose presence is merely tolerated, and a licensee by invitation, or a social guest. Although a social guest may be invited and even urged to come, they are not an invitee with the legal meaning of that term. A social guest is no more than a licensee who is expected to accept the premises in the same manner as the owner uses the property.[55]

A person who enters undeveloped land without paying a fee is owed the least amount of care to make the premises safe.

TRESPASSER

A trespasser is defined as someone who intentionally or without consent or privilege enters another's property.[56] The word "trespasser" is commonly used for anyone falling under that definition and does not necessarily imply any illegal act. A person who goes upon publicly owned land to enjoy a hike or wander the land is a "technical" trespasser, but certainly has not committed a criminal act of trespass.

Example: A hiker on a National Forest broke his ankle when he stepped into a wild animal hole adjacent to the trail. He did not pay a fee, was not specifically invited, and

had no business or commerce purposes in the park visit. He would be considered a trespasser under the definition of the word. Therefore, in the legal application of this category of user, he would qualify as a technical trespasser. Because of his visitor status, he would unlikely be able to pursue a successful suit.

Owners, operators, and managers owe adult trespassers a duty of care less than that of a licensee. They have no duty to make their property or facilities reasonably safe or to warn of dangerous conditions. They only have a duty to avoid injury by intentional, reckless, and wanton misconduct.

SPECIAL CATEGORY OF VISITOR

There may be a question as to the status of the non-fee-paying person who enters a public park to view flowers, play ball, have a picnic, or use the park in a number of ways that are compatible with the park's intent. Essentially the visitor was invited, enticed, or attracted to the facility or activity. While the person is a "technical trespasser," the courts will view these individuals in an "in-between" status and consider other standards as they relate to the care owed the visitor. They are sometimes defined as public invitees or simply non-paying visitors who are on the premises at the invitation or enticement of the owner.

Example: An agency is the sponsor of a widely advertised native craft exhibition. Hundreds of people attend the event from all over the state. A fee is charged by the exhibitor if a purchase is made; however, the public is allowed into the exhibition free of charge. Agency officials must recognize that because of the enticing advertisements, the visitors would enjoy a status above that of a legal trespasser, but not necessarily to the level of a paid invitee. Such a visitor would at a minimum be owed a higher level of care and must be warned of any known dangers.

ATTRACTIVE NUISANCE

Children are by nature curious and have very little sense of potential danger. Children may trespass upon property because new or unusual environments are both adventurous and exciting. The law provides

Special measures are necessary when properties contain features particularly attractive to children.

words "attractive nuisance" may not be used in some jurisdictions, having been replaced by the "foreseeability doctrine," but the important principle still remains—children fit into a separate category when it comes to the trespass category of visitors.

Example: A public recreation property maintains a fishing pond in the middle of its property. The park closes to the public during the winter months and posts signs indicating that the area is closed—no trespassing. There are a number of children who live near the park in a suburban neighborhood. Children commonly go into the park for sledding and ice skating on the pond. A child falls through the ice and is drowned. The property owner would be subject to suit because he knew children were trespassing, and the owner should have reasonably determined (it was foreseeable) that there were times that the children would be endangered by thin ice.

RECREATION LAND-USE STATUTES

In recent years almost all states have enacted recreational land-use statutes that provide some protection to public and private landowners who allow their property to be used for public recreation purposes without a fee. The recreation land-use statutes seldom apply when attractive nuisance is involved. A careful analysis of the individual state statutes is important to the application of these statutes to a trespasser. See Chapter 1 for further information on recreation land use.

protection for the mischievous child seeking out a place to hide or play. Warning signs have no impact on the non-reader, and decorative fences are meant to be climbed in the eyes of children. In the case of trespassing children, the attractive nuisance doctrine applies. Essentially, owners who have created artificial or man-made conditions where common sense indicates that children may trespass, or where the land possesses something that may be expected to attract children, are under duty to provide such care as a reasonably prudent person would take to prevent injury. These provisions usually do not apply to natural conditions, only to artificial conditions. The

4

Employee Rights

KEYWORDS

Constitutional guarantees   *EEO policy*   *Employee Rights*
Protection of Public Employees   *Title VII, Civil Rights Act* *Equal Pay Act*
Employee Recruitment   *Firing*

The purpose of this chapter is to point out some of the pitfalls to avoid in managing employee rights. Following this chapter you should have a good understanding of:

1. *What the U.S. Constitution guarantees in the way of employee rights*
2. *What protections you and your employees have through constitutional rights*
3. *How Title VII of the Civil Rights Act deals with civil employment relationships*
4. *Understand some of the intricacies of recruitment, selection, and placement of new employees*
5. *How to fire an employee and the required documentation*

An area of increasing concern and risk for the park, recreation, and leisure service manager is related to employment rights established and guaranteed through the U.S. Constitution and other federal and state and employment and civil rights-related legislation. The Constitution establishes specific guaranteed rights such as due process and freedom of speech that affect employee relationships. In addition, employees may also have selective employee benefits established through professional societies, employment (labor) contracts, and union agreements. A wise manager will ensure that employees are treated in a manner that respects their legal rights and provides for equal and fair treatment in all their activities. Managers are particularly vulnerable in the recruitment, employee evaluation, new employee selection, evaluation, retention, and when necessary, the termination of employees.

The U.S. Constitution is applicable to everyone in every jurisdiction. State constitutions only apply to their own states and their provisions do not supersede the provisions of the U.S. Constitution. A local constitution or charter applies only to the local governmental entity. If there is a conflict among the various laws, the federal laws control and have predominance over state and local laws.

This chapter will point out some of the pitfalls to avoid in managing these rights and offer some suggestions on how to cope with these concerns based on existing laws, case studies, and common sense.

The legal implications of employee hiring and firing are stringent and getting more complex. Make certain everyone in the organization's chain is familiar with equal employment opportunity laws and federal and state employment regulations.

CONSTITUTIONAL GUARANTEES

The founding fathers of the Untied States determined, as they drafted the Bill of Rights, that all citizens would be afforded specific rights. Some of the constitutional rights most often affecting recreation and leisure participants, visitors, and employees are as follows:

1. The First Amendment gives citizens the rights of free speech and religion. The first amendment also protects citizens from excessive government intrusion into private matters. Within the context of the first amendment is the separation or division of church and state. Government entities cannot establish policies that prefer one religion over another or establish a "state church."[57] The First Amendment of the Constitution protects the rights of citizens to assemble, to petition their government, and to be heard by their government representatives and agencies. Citizens have a right to attend most policy-related meetings and voice their opinions.

2. The Fourth Amendment provides protection from unreasonable searches and seizures and the requirement of a search warrant, except in special circumstances such as immediate pursuit of a suspected criminals. Generally, an employer cannot search a locked desk or locker without the permission of the user/occupier.

3. The Fifth Amendment protects the citizen's right to life, liberty, and to own property. These rights cannot be circumvented or taken away without due process of the law. This amendment also provides that private property cannot be taken for public use without compensating the owner. Taking property by the government is commonly called the "Right of

The requirements of due process cover many aspects of our society.

Eminent Domain." The taking of property for government purposes such as roads has been supported by decisions of the U.S. Supreme Court; however, taking private lands for private economic develop is rapidly developing into a major controversial issue.

4. The Tenth Amendment gives all police powers to the states and local governments not specifically retained by the federal government. Only a few federal jurisdictions such as land owned by the military, Indian reservations, and some selected National Parks (i.e., Yellowstone) maintain full federal control of the land and its use through federal statutes. With few exceptions, the states and counties retain law enforcement jurisdiction for the enforcement of state law and local ordinances.

5. The Fourteenth Amendment limits the power of state and local government so they can not pass laws that supersede the federal laws. As an example, if the federal government declares an area off limits

to motorized vehicles, the state or local government cannot pass a law in opposition to the federal law that opens the area to vehicles.

Violation of the above U.S. Constitutional Amendments has serious and important consequences related to the management of recreation properties, employee relations, and visitor/user rights.

Example: A public agency receptionist arrives one day with a small crucifix around her neck. The following weeks she is wearing a very large crucifix around her neck. The next week she is still wearing the large crucifix around her neck and has added a crucifix on a stand on her desk. The next week she has the crucifix around her neck, the crucifix on her desk and has placed a few religious brochures on the receptionist counter. When asked to remove the materials she indicates that freedom of expression and freedom of religion are protected by the First Amendment to the Constitution. What is your response?

Most managers will face a dilemma such as the situation above sometime in their career. The First Amendment to the Constitution, referred to as the establishment clause, forbids laws that prohibit free exercise and also forbids laws that would establish or sponsor a religion. Anytime individual religious expression appears to indicate sponsorship by an agency or organization, the constitutional issue of separation of church and state emerges. Neither the federal government nor the states and their subdivisions can set up or sponsor a church. Neither can they pass laws which favor one religion over another.[55] In the example given, the personal expression of religion through the wearing of a crucifix should be protected; however, when the employee placed the crucifix on her desk, the symbol of belief becomes connected with agency property, not a specific person. A subtle message is sent to the public that the recreation agency is sponsoring a single religious belief.

EEO POLICY STATEMENT

Most park, recreation, and leisure service organizations have an equal-opportunity employment policy statement that represents the ethical and legal standards of their community. If an organization does not have an equal opportunity policy, consideration should be made to adopt a statement similar to the following:

"We the ____(agency name)____, are an equal-employment opportunity employer for all persons regardless of race, creed, color, age, national origin, marital status, or disability. We will vigorously enforce a policy of employment based solely on ability, qualifications, merit, and physical capability. Our executives, managers, and supervisors will be held accountable for carrying out this policy."

EMPLOYEE RIGHTS

While there are a number of rights established by statutes and the U.S. Constitution; there remains a great deal of discretionary or optional areas that should be part of the employment contract and employee organization (i.e., union) agreements. Some of the more controversial subject areas such as safety, dress standards, behavior standards, compensation, work hours, overtime compensation, and benefits should be specifically covered in employment documents that are reviewed by the employee and documented in writing.

PROTECTION OF PUBLIC EMPLOYEES

Public employees are protected through Constitutional Rights (see above) as well as legislation and case law. The following categories are legal areas for managers and administrators to exercise particular attention to insure equal protection:

Alienage

Employers must protect the rights of their employees and visitors in regard to their place of birth and citizenship. Just because a person was born in another country or does not have U.S. citizenship does not automatically disqualify him from employment.[58]

Race

Employers must insure there is no bias in regard to their employees' and visitors' racial background,

An administrator can be sued for discriminatory hiring practices.

including African-American, Asian-American, Native American, Caucasian, and other racial classifications. Some racial discrimination is subtle and very difficult to identify; however, over time it will be discovered and usually results in expensive appeals and litigation. Supervisors and administrators should make special efforts to eliminate any part of an operation that may in any way be discriminatory.[59]

Religion

Employees and the public need protection of their rights in regard to religious beliefs, or creed. The rights to religious beliefs balanced by the need to separate church and state are basic to U.S. culture. Respecting belief without favoring specific religions is a balancing act necessary for all supervisors and administrators.[60]

Gender

Protection of rights in regard to gender (male/female) issues must be continually monitored. In most jurisdictions gender protection is not extended into sexual orientation issues and generally relates to equal treatment of both men and women in the workplace.[61]

Pregnancy

Protection of parents' rights prior to, during, and after child bearing must be protected. Most common issues involve leave, job protection, and seniority questions. Women cannot be discriminated against because "just after we train her, she will get pregnant and be off work a number of months." Through both federal and state laws, fathers have some limited employee and leave rights related to the birth of their children established by statute.[62]

Age

Rights related to age limits on jobs must be protected. Age classification protection usually does not include rights of minor children, but rather, discrimination in hiring, retention, and firing because of age. In most cases the issue should be physical and mental ability rather than age. In a physical-ability situation, the employment criteria should involve physical fitness to perform and not age. There is specific job protection for people between the ages of forty (40) and seventy (70). Employers should recognize the limitations placed upon hiring young people under the age of 18 while they are still in school. Small family-owned and -run businesses (such as farms) are usually exempt from work-age limitations.[63]

Physical or Mental Handicaps

Law protects the rights of those with physical and mental limitations from exploitation or unwarranted harassment. Many employers claim some of their most dependable and hard-working employees are physically or mentally disabled. Employment standards that arbitrarily eliminate these categories from consideration for jobs and advancement are unacceptable.[64]

Residency

Protection must be given to people not living in a specified area that would limit their participation in public-sponsored activities and employment. Extra fees, such as additional camping fees, can be collected from participants outside of the taxing jurisdiction, but people cannot be completely excluded from work and access to public recreation facilities because of the place of residence.[65]

Speech

People must be protected from harassment or denial of employment opportunities because of an individual exercise of free speech. People should not be punished because they disagree or have controversial opinions. An employee's right to state his concerns and disagreements must be maintained; however, disruptive and unlawful speech behavior is not protected.[66]

Association

The rights of people who associate with others who may be deemed by society as undesirable must be protected. Participation in protest marches, political association, or other expressive behavior cannot be the basis of employment retaliation. U.S. government workers are also protected from agency retaliation after "whistle blowing."[67]

Privacy and Liberty of Choice
in Personal Matters

People should be protected from an organization's "prying eyes" unless such intrusions are necessary for safety, behavior requirements, or agreed to in writing by the employee. A person's home life, as long as it is not illegal, is separated from a person's business life. Only those behaviors that bring direct criticism on an agency or organization as a result of employee behavior should be of concern to the employer.[68]

(Please note that the endnote references related to the above protected classes indicate important, precedent-setting litigation.)

Exceptions

There are some exceptions to equal rights protection such as employment in private clubs and religious organizations. Concerns related to security clearances may also be an exception. In addition, there are some legislated exceptions such as veterans' preference in employment superseding the required

diversity to meet women and minorities balances and classifications.

TITLE VII OF THE CIVIL RIGHTS ACT OF 1964

Title VII of the Civil Rights Act deals with discrimination in the employment relationship and covers organizations with 15 or more employees. It does not apply to religious organizations, Indian tribes, and private membership clubs. As a general guide affirmative action (§703 [i]) programs should require a "community snap-shot" of racial and ethic representation in a workforce that is comparable to the area population. Exceptions (defenses) to this requirement includes:

1. Bona Fide Occupational Qualifications (§ 703 [e]). If an organization needs a computer programmer, the decision of hiring should be based on the

qualifications of the applicants. Protected classes of people are not given consideration unless they meet bona fide qualifications.

2. Seniority(§ 703 [h]). An organization can pay a person more than another if they have worked for the company or in a position for a longer period of time. (See Equal Pay Act requirements)

3. Good Faith Reliance (§ 713 [b]). If a organization has a plan to meet integration standards and have an absence of malice and absence of a design to defraud they can be declared as having "good faith reliance."

4. Undue Hardship (§ 701 [j]). If meeting Civil Rights Act requirements results in more damage than good for a community or people in general, the organization can defend their actions by declaring an "undue hardship."

5. Religious Practice (§ 702). Because of the guarantees of freedom of religion, religious organizations can defend their actions on the basis of religious practice.

As an example: A religious organization can have as part of their religious beliefs that clergy is male.

6. Other Statutory Defenses.

   a. Veterans' Preference (§ 712). In most federal government jobs qualified veterans are given five or 10 points on their unassembled examinations. Some states also have statutory provisions that favor veterans.

   b. Security Clearances (§ 703 [g]). Some sensitive jobs require security clearances. Regardless of an individual classification they still must meet security requirements for employment.

   c. Communists (§ 703 [fl]). The communist classification is still part of the law; however, it is very hard to find a pro claimed communist not to hire today.

When the courts determine that employment discrimination has in fact taken place, the courts have a number of remedies available to them.[69] They are as follows:

1. Injunctive Relief–Court directed hiring or reinstatement.

2. Monetary Relief–Cash payment to the grieving party(s).

3. Remedial Seniority–Advancing a person's seniority to compensate for past discrimination.

4. Attorney's Fees–Requiring the defendant to pay the attorney fees of the plaintiff.

5. Affirmative Action–A court-directed plan that will provide opportunities for those who have been previously discriminated against.

EQUAL PAY ACT

The Equal Pay Act[70] provides that employers cannot discriminate between employees doing the same work on the basis of gender. The enforcement and remedies for this act are provided through the National Labor Relations Act.[71] Violation of the Equal Pay Act (pay discrimination by gender) has serious consequences.

Provisions of the Equal Pay Act include:

1. The act's provisions can be enforced by both public court actions and private suits.

2. Back wages can be awarded.

3. If found guilty of pay discrimination, employers will pay both compensatory and punitive damages.

4. All suits must be filed within two years of the incident; however, if the plaintiff can prove the discrimination was willful, the suit may be filed within three years.

5. If the plaintiff wins the suit, the defendant employer must pay all attorney fees.

6. There can be no penalty or retaliation against an employee who files a Equal Pay Act grievance.

It is obvious that employers must be very careful to insure equal pay for equal work. The employer does have some legal defenses for pay discrimination suits.

Defenses include:

1. *Seniority*—Persons can be paid more that have more time with the organization or in a specific job classification.

2. *Merit*—Persons can be paid more if through education or training they are more skilled at their tasks.

3. *Production (quality or quantity)*—If through documentation a person is a higher producer or does more quality work they can be paid more.

4. *Differences not based upon gender*—If significant measured differences can be established that would normally be part of work requirements or are safety related, then compensation can vary.

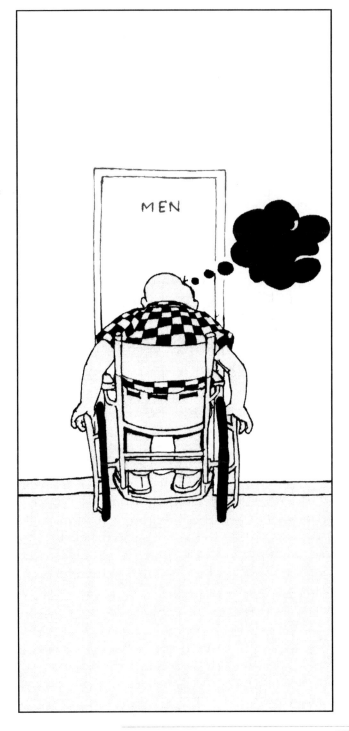

OTHER ACTS RELATED TO EMPLOYMENT AND SERVICES

Age Discrimination in Employment Act of 1967

Provides for the protection of older citizens from age discrimination.

Rehabilitation Act of 1973[72]

Provides for changes in architectural design to facilitate the disabled citizens relating to new construction and major remodeling and upgrading.[73]

The Americans with Disabilities Act of 1990

Provides for a broad range of access to work, school, and public facilities for those with disabilities.[74]

Fair Labor Standards Act

The act provides that subject to some exceptions, persons working in interstate commerce must be paid not less than the federally mandated minimum wage and they cannot be employed for more than 40 hours a week unless they are paid time and a half for overtime. This act also prohibits the employment of children under the age of 14 years. It permits the employment of children between the ages of 14 and 16 years in some selected industries.[75]

Hours of Service Act

Regulates those driving a common carrier (freight truck, bus, cab, etc.) or other public transportation cannot work over 16 consecutive hours or within 10 hours thereafter, or within eight hours after 16 hours of labor within any 24-hour period. Some modes of public transportation have more stringent rules, such as the airline industry.

Occupational Safety and Health Act[76]

Provides for federal safety standards for most activities.

Federal Freedom of Information Act of 1974[77]

Allows the public to gain access to most public meetings and public records. Exceptions include working papers, legal preparations, and properly classified secret or confidential materials and records.[78]

Federal Privacy Act of 1974

Provides that people cannot gain access into records that are private in nature, such as medical and personnel records.[79]

EMPLOYEE RECRUITMENT

Job Description—Recruitment generally starts with the preparation of a job description. One should

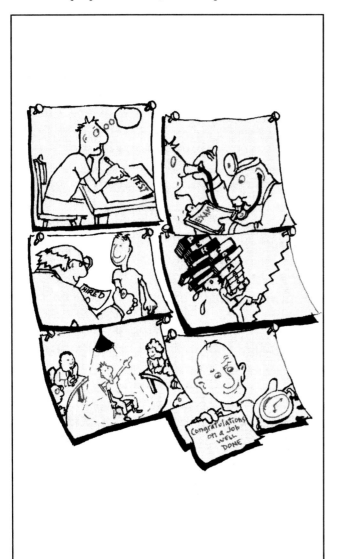

avoid references to age, sex, race, religion, and citizenship. A requirement to enclose a photograph could well provide information on a person's age, sex, and race and should be avoided. It is appropriate to include position title, to whom the person reports, a summary of the job, duties and responsibilities, experience required, educational requirements, physical requirements, salary and/or hourly wage ranges, and benefit packages. To avoid confusion in the future about job responsibilities, there should be a summary paragraph that states "the above description and list of duties and responsibilities is a general guide only and are not to be considered as an implied or written contract."

Employment Application Form—There are a number of items that should be asked and a number of things that *should not* be asked on an employment application form. For example, asking the applicant's place of birth may reduce the opportunities of a foreign-born applicant. Questions related to place of birth may be applicable for many governmental jobs, however, if it is not legally necessary to ask the questions, they should not be asked. Sensitive questions should not be asked verbally either. Generally, applications should be kept for a period of one year, unless a disclaimer is placed on the application stating that the application will be kept for a specific period of time, such as 60 days.

GUIDELINES ON APPLICATIONS:

It may be inappropriate to ask:
1. A person's gender
2. A person's marital status
3. Maiden name
4. Age
5. Height and weight
6. Education (unless job related)
7. Has person applied for Workmen's Compensation
8. Prior misdemeanor arrests not related to job
9. Union or organization affiliation
10. Language used in home
11. Religion
12. Sexual preferences
13. Ownership of car or home
14. Race

15. Where parents or spouse were born
16. Disabilities
17. Financial condition

You should ask about:
1. Position applied for
2. Social security number
3. Prior military service
4. Why the applicant may not perform any of the job duties
5. Previous criminal felony convictions
6. English language skills
7. Travel restrictions or objections
8. Overtime restrictions or objections
9. Objections to Saturday or Sunday work
10. Drug use, past or present
11. Work history of applicant
12. Permission to contact former employers
13. Job-related skills and knowledge
14. Education

It should be noted that you cannot eliminate a disabled person from consideration unless the person's disability affects job performance. As a general rule, you cannot ask women anything you cannot ask men and vice versa.

SELECTION

Some of the tools used in making the final selection are: Testing, checking references, and interviewing.

Testing

Testing job candidates can, if not very carefully done, become a legal minefield.

It is important to remember that it is the agency's responsibility, not the responsibility of the testing company to make absolutely certain that whatever testing procedure is used, it meets all the criteria established by the EEO.

When using tests, remember any test used as part of hiring must be related to the specific job for which the applicant has applied. Secondly, the nature of the questions asked cannot reduce the chance of

women and minorities being hired. If questioned about test content you must be able to show that the testing procedure represents a reasonable way of predicting job performance. Similarly, if challenged to defend a charge of discrimination against minorities or females you must be able to show a correlation between high test scores and good on-the-job performance.

There are tests available that cover job skills, intelligence, integrity, attitudes toward theft, violence, drugs, and much more. Tests must be administered consistently and fairly. Where possible, as in the case of testing lifeguards, you may choose to simulate actual job-related situations by having applications demonstrate their abilities in and around the water resource for which you are recruiting. Tests should be validated by competent authorities. You may want to consider, in the case of lifeguard testing, having the local chapter of the American Red Cross certify the list of qualified applicants.

Medical examinations are a form of testing and if required, should be part of the information given on the application form. Such examinations can be used to establish benchmarks for workers compensation and to disqualify applicants if there are medical reasons why individuals should not be employed.

References

Reference checking is an important part of recruitment and the recruitment process. It is necessary to verify the information furnished by the applicant. Applicants should be informed that references will be checked since it will help match their job skills with the position advertised.

When applicants for a position are rejected it is sufficient to say, "The position for which you applied has been filled." If pressured to give a reason you may choose to say, "We hired the person whom we felt had the best qualifications for the position." If the rejection is related to the applicant's education and or experience, skills, or work requirements you may tell them that information.

When actually hiring the individual, it is well to describe what is now commonly called an introductory or probationary period. Avoid using the words "permanent employee;" rather use the words "full-time employee."

Interviewing

Effective interviewing is a learned skill. One of the first principles of good job interviewing is knowing as much as possible about the position being filled. One of the most common pitfalls in ineffective interviews is talking too much instead of listening. An interviewer should listen at least 70 percent of the time. Silence may be used as a tool to evoke comments from the interviewee. Avoid the tendency to hire people "just like you." Work at not settling for the mediocre employee. Don't oversell the job or your organization, and don't promise "everything" to prospective employees.

There are some key questions to ask during the interviewing process. These questions are designed to give you and your organization an insight into the applicant's personality in a short period of time. Remember that you may not be able to ask the sensitive questions noted in the "applications" section of this chapter (see p. 38). It is good interviewing technique for the applicant to watch you take notes as he or she speaks. Robert Half states: "Asking the right questions takes as much skill as giving the right answers."

KEY QUESTIONS

Why do you think we should hire you?

What do you think your last supervisor will tell me are your two weakest areas and your two greatest strengths?

Why did you leave your last job?

Tell me, in detail, what you did the day before yesterday.

What makes you different from the others applying for this job?

Where does the power come from in your organization?

What specific strengths would you bring to the organization?

Why have you decided to leave your present position?

Where would you like to be three years from now?

Tell me about your hobbies and interests.

What were your best subjects in school?

Why did you go or not go to college?

How would you describe your academic achievement?

What have you done about your own skill development in the last few years?

What was your major accomplishment in your last position?

In general, how would you describe yourself?

What do you think is behind your success?

EMPLOYEE PERFORMANCE EVALUATION

Employee performance evaluations are used for a number of purposes. They can be used to encourage positive feedback from employees, change poor performance, be the basis for promotion or dismissal, and provide the legal justification for other actions. There are a number of court cases each year related to performance evaluation. The following are some of the items that need the attention of administrators, managers, and supervisors[80] (Note—endnotes refer to important legal cases that have established the standard of care required for each category.):

1. Equal Policy Enforcement—Each employee should be evaluated in a specific time period each year. Failure to evaluate employees and thus denying them the opportunity for promotion may subject an organization to litigation.[81]

2. Use of Improper Evaluation Criteria—Evaluation should be related to the evaluation criteria es-

tablished upon employment or at the latest evaluation session. Using additional criteria is inappropriate.[82]

3. Communication of Private Information—Communications between an employer and a employee should not include a third person not involved with the issues. The so-called "water fountain" conversations that may be either defamatory or factual involving private information or performance evaluation can be subject to litigation because of a person's right to privacy. There is a "need to know" concept that should be part of communicating any information involving job performance.[83]

4. Prior Discussion of Performance Requirements—Supervisors should discuss performance requirements with their employees prior to evaluation. Sometimes a hesitant supervisor does not want to "hurt the feelings" of a employee by discussing poor performance when it occurs. Employees should be given the opportunity to change behavior at the earliest time possible.[84]

5. Inadequate Rater Training—All raters should be trained using the same criteria. Objective methods must be used to insure that a "easy" rater's employees do not get all the performance-based promotions in his/her unit while the more critical rater's subordinates are not considered for promotion.

6. Minority Representation on Rating Boards—Minorities (i.e., race, gender, age, etc.) should be represented on rating teams. The raters should represent the diversity of the workforce.[85]

7. Rating System Should Be Monitored—Management should insure that the rating system is being properly utilized and that safeguards to guard its integrity are in place. There should also be a formal appeal process.

FIRING

There are many reasons why firing someone is just plain distasteful. It goes against our human nature and compassion. We are reluctant to dismiss someone because do not like to talk about someone's failure or admit that we personally failed to implement changes that would have positively changed the employee's performance. We may be concerned about a lawsuit. Our dislike for firing may result in our keeping unproductive and problem employees who might perform much better in a different environment. We do not realize that firing a difficult or unproductive employee will do a favor for both the organization and the individual being fired.

Firing people has become more difficult, but we must not fall prey to thinking that it is an impossible task. When it comes time to let someone go who is simply not performing to the organization's satisfaction, we suggest the following approach:

1. Do the firing yourself. If the employee works for you, it is a management problem that you cannot delegate.

2. Let the employee know verbally and in writing that his performance is unsatisfactory. Have them sign an employee counseling statement to the effect that they have received a notice of reprimand. Make it very clear that the person's job is in jeopardy. Establish a reasonable time limit for improvement.

3. Suspend if necessary. Do it verbally and in writing.

4. Give a final warning in writing.

5. Finally terminate. Termination should be done in a non-public manner that allows the separated employee some dignity and respect.

It is important to have a rather short firing process. A long process places a great deal of stress on all individuals involved. Supervisors should be prepared for bad reactions, dealing with pleas, and personal threats. Finally, a supervisor must be cautious about writing a glowing reference for an undeserving dismissed employee. These references can be used as evidence of unfair termination.

DOCUMENT/DOCUMENT/DOCUMENT

In all matters involving employee rights and performance evaluation, wise supervisors will thoroughly document all conversations, complaints, and actions taken. It is particularly important to have detailed records of behavior problems, absenteeism, substance abuse, and sexual harassment complaints. All resignations should be in writing, dated, and signed. This becomes particularly important when civil rights violations may be involved or future adverse action may be necessary. Any change or improvement in work should be made in writing. The letter or memorandum of dismissal should document an "earlier conversation."

It is probably a rare occasion when an employee who is about to be terminated does not realize that he/she is in trouble. It has been said that employees fire themselves, not the other way around. Yet it is still an unpleasant task. The final decision will be easier if the supervisor:

1. Has well-documented reason for the dismissal
2. Gives the employee adequate warning
3. Never fires out of anger
4. Is certain of the decision
5. Is prepared for a difficult reaction
6. Does it in a timely manner
7. Is honest, not ruthless
8. Is sensitive to the employee's needs
9. Knows the organization's termination policies, i.e., final pay, insurance, etc.
10. Does not promise something out of sympathy that cannot be delivered

As a final comment, a person who is dismissed is owed the specific reasons for their dismissal so they can change their behavior and find future success in employment. It is a cruel act indeed if the person who was fired was not told the truth about his dismissal.

5

The Risk-Management Plan

<table>
<tr><td colspan="3">Key Words</td></tr>
<tr><td>Risk</td><td>Needs assessment</td><td>Responsibility</td></tr>
<tr><td>Supervision</td><td>Authority</td><td>Inspections</td></tr>
<tr><td>Authorization</td><td>Investigations</td><td>Monitoring</td></tr>
<tr><td>Accident reporting</td><td>Policy</td><td>Emergency procedures</td></tr>
<tr><td>Goals and objectives</td><td>Risk insurance</td><td>Rules</td></tr>
<tr><td>In-service training</td><td>Regulations</td><td>Public relations</td></tr>
<tr><td>Procedures</td><td>Periodic review</td><td></td></tr>
</table>

The purpose of this chapter is to lay the groundwork for establishing a comprehensive plan to manage risk in your agency. Following this chapter you should be able to:

1. *Develop a solid risk management plan based on the 16 steps to managing risk*
2. *Understand the importance of managing risk for your board members, your staff, and the users of your facilities*
3. *Reduce losses from potential liability suits filed against your agency*
4. *Organize and keep track of claims, losses, and insurance coverages*
5. *Provide a public relations program regarding risk that enhances your agency in the eyes of the general public*

WHY HAVE A PLAN?

With a risk-management plan, you will be taking a proactive approach to managing risk. You will project an attitude that says:

"Yes, we are knowledgeable professionals, we are concerned for your safety, and we will do what is necessary to provide a safe environment for your leisure activities."

In addition to doing what is professionally sound, a risk-management plan is extremely valuable in the event of legal action against your organization. A solidly proactive program shows intent. A program of managing risk serves as a deterrent to being sued and, if sued, as evidence of intent to act responsibly.

Other benefits include:

1. Increased safety for the consumers of your services
2. Reduced losses to your organization
3. More effective use of available funds
4. Identifies exposures you can cover through an alternative to insurance
5. Makes your organization more attractive to insurance companies
6. Reduces uncertainties associated with future projects
7. Keeps track of claims, losses, and insurance coverage

WHO IS RESPONSIBLE FOR THE PLAN?

Many of the accidents that occur daily can be prevented. The National Safety Council says that 85 percent of all accidents are preventable. The fact is the many accidents that might have occurred are being prevented or severely reduced in severity by those managerial teams who develop and execute a program of risk management focusing on reasonable care.

Sounds almost too simple, doesn't it?

The challenge comes in understanding the procedure, the reasons why we do something, and who is responsible. Consider the following questions as the risk-management plan begins to unfold:

1. Who authorizes the plan?
2. Who develops it?
3. Who carries it out?
4. What is in the plan?

Before addressing the "what," let's describe the "who." Who is responsible for the plan? There is an old adage that says, "Everyone's responsibility is no one's responsibility." There is a little irony in that statement when it comes to managing risk, because for such a plan to be effective everyone in the organization needs to be involved. It does, however, take the constant effort of a key coordinator to assist, guide, train, motivate, and consult with staff throughout the system to accomplish the agency's goals.

Figure 1 illustrates everyone's responsibility. Regardless of agency size, any risk management plan should have the blessing and authority of the governing body, particularly of policy-making boards. That body may be a public park and recreation board or commission, an agency board of the YMCA or Boy's Club, a school board, or a private corporation governing body. The establishment of a policy by the governing or corporate authority legitimizes their position

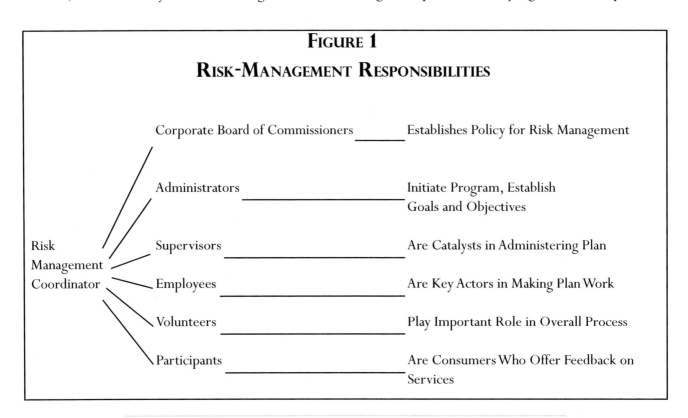

FIGURE 1
RISK-MANAGEMENT RESPONSIBILITIES

Corporate Board of Commissioners	Establishes Policy for Risk Management
Administrators	Initiate Program, Establish Goals and Objectives
Supervisors	Are Catalysts in Administering Plan
Employees	Are Key Actors in Making Plan Work
Volunteers	Play Important Role in Overall Process
Participants	Are Consumers Who Offer Feedback on Services

Risk Management Coordinator

and tells the staff and users that they believe in the concept. By authorizing and ultimately approving the plan, the governing body is making its statement for responsibility in managing risk.

The administrator's role is to carry out the wishes of the board or governing authority and determine the best method to develop and monitor a risk management plan. The size of the department or agency will be a determining factor. In smaller units, the administrator may be responsible. In larger units, a risk management officer may be assigned on a full-time basis. In most departments, however, the duty will be coupled with other administrative functions. In larger units with a fully maintained program, the duties would include at least the following responsibilities:

1. Full coordination responsibility for safety.
2. Identify risk management problem areas and recommending corrective action.
3. Prepare risk management budget, including insurance, safety, and loss prevention controls, and authorizing necessary expenditures.
4. Stay informed of local, state, and federal court decisions, rules, regulations, and statutes.
5. Establish, maintain, and supervise an agency-wide program of employee safety and loss prevention.
6. Establish claims reporting and maintaining procedures.
7. Work with legal counsel and the insurance broker constantly to monitor, supervise, and administer the overall program.
8. Establish insurance requirements for vendors and contractors doing business with the agency and approve all contracts regarding compliance with requirements.

The key point to remember is that it must be someone's responsibility, or it ends up being no one's obligation. The administrator's role doesn't end with the appointment of a risk management officer. One must be willing to release proper authority allowing the officer to carry out such duties as initiating safety meetings, training programs, inspections, investigations, and general supervision of the program. The successful administrator will make a statement of responsibility by:

1. Establishing goals
2. Assigning responsibility
3. Releasing authority
4. Encouraging feedback
5. Monitoring progress

Supervisors play a vital role in risk management planning and execution. The supervisor generally has the most influence and control over employee work habits and attitudes. The "on-site" supervisor is familiar with the day-to-day work environment and is in a critical position to affect the outcome of any risk management plan.

Management's challenge is to involve supervisory staff in a total commitment to safety and risk management—a commitment that stems from understanding and belief in the value of such a system. The personal support of an enthusiastic supervisor spurs the "action" that takes any program beyond the paper. A supervisor's duties include:

1. Serve on the safety committee.
2. Train employees to work safely.
3. Discuss safety with individual employees.
4. Correct unsafe conditions and unsafe acts.
5. Report and investigate accidents to help determine cause.
6. Inspect work areas for compliance with safe work practices and rules.

Finally, in the hierarchy of involvement, all employees below the supervisory level, plus volunteers and participants, must be included in the process of developing a risk-management plan.

Employees are credited with being the first to recognize on-the-job hazards. Their work brings them in daily contact with many potentially dangerous facilities or equipment, and they should be praised for frequently having excellent suggestions for improving or correcting unsafe conditions.

It is not always easy to capitalize on employee skills and knowledge. Unless they understand "what's in it for them" and become committed in the same manner as their supervisors, they may perceive the new wave of regulations as just another top-down obligation imposed by the administration. They could care less! Meaningful involvement of administrators and supervisors can be the elixir that stimulates other employees to join the effort.

In developing a comprehensive risk-management plan, the volunteers in particular must be part of the process. As we have learned earlier, volunteers are subject to legal actions against them in a manner similar to regular paid employees. It is important to treat volunteers as an integral part of the staff. *Certification of coaches and leaders in their areas of specialty is an important aspect of risk management.*

You can add credibility to your risk-management plan by asking for input from your volunteers. Invite volunteers to join some of the task forces working on the project and involve participants through telephone surveys, questionnaires, or personal interviews. Any plan encouraging such techniques will be strengthened.

DEVELOPING THE PLAN

It is virtually impossible to design a plan comprehensive enough to serve all purposes. It would be foolhardy to think that if each step were followed precisely, there would be no tort liability. The system doesn't work that way. What we are saying is that the courts have, over time, looked favorably upon certain management practices in tort liability cases. There is nothing magic about this plan. Many departments are already practicing the various tasks described, perhaps without realizing that they may already have a plan. In that case, the outline will allow you to review your current practices and improve them wherever possible. For those initiating a comprehensive plan, the outline will allow for the logical sequencing of events so that you may say this is our approach to managing risk, our plan, if you will, to act responsibly.

SIXTEEN STEPS TO MANAGING RISK

1. Philosophy/Policy Statements
2. Needs Assessment
3. Goals and Objectives
4. Site and Facility Development
5. Program Development
6. Supervision
7. Establishment of Rules, Regulations, and Procedures

8. Safety Inspections and Investigations
9. Accident Reporting and Analysis
10. Emergency Procedures
11. Releases, Waivers, and Agreements to Participate
12. Methods of Insuring Against Risk
13. In-service Training
14. Public Relations
15. Outside Specialists, Legal/Insurance
16. Periodic Review

Step 1. Philosophy/Policy Statements

Task—Develop philosophical and policy statements regarding your organization's belief in developing a risk-management loss prevention and control program. This is the opportunity for the governing authority to get involved and stay involved. The governing authority should express its commitment by adopting a philosophy of risk management and by approving policy statements as they are developed.

Philosophy defined—A critical examination of the grounds for fundamental beliefs and an analysis of the basic concepts employed in the expression of such beliefs. (*Webster's 3rd International Dictionary*)

Suggested approach
1. Review your existing philosophical statements found in ordinances, charters, master plans, and administrative manuals.
2. Key words to consider in developing a philosophy of risk management:
    a. aim or purpose
    b. endorsement
    c. qualified leaders
    d. commitment
    e. services
    f. reasonable care
3. Formulate your ideas into a specific statement related to managing risk.
4. Have your governing authority formally adopt the statement.

Sample Risk-Management Philosophy

To: All Employees
From: Governing Authority
Subject: Our Risk-Management Philosophy

It is the basic purpose of the (name of jurisdiction) to establish, improve, manage, and finance the park system. We are committed to a philosophy that will provide these services at the highest level possible. We pledge our support to using only qualified and trained leaders in accord with the best and most reasonable standard of care possible. To that end, we endorse the establishment and maintenance of an extensive program to manage risk safely within the organization.

Policy defined—A definite course or method of action to guide and determine present and future decisions.

Suggested approach—It is desirable, in fact essential, to have written policies and procedures for reporting accidents, conducting field trips, establishing what records to keep, determining what fees and charges will be made, deciding who must register, etc.

In developing policies, the governing authority should adopt a brief policy statement of a general nature as the basis for formulating a policy and ask the administrative staff to develop detailed guidelines for their approval.

Example: A general policy statement might be as follows: "It is the policy of (name of jurisdiction) to require parental permission slips for all youth programs."

How to proceed
1. Ask a committee of your governing board or administrative staff or some combination of the two to draft a statement for review.
2. Appoint a risk manager (coordinator) on a temporary or permanent basis and ask this person to prepare a draft.
3. Seek advice of your legal counsel, your insurance broker, or individuals with special knowledge, such as a risk manager for a local industry.

4. Adopt a provisional statement and modify it later as your knowledge of risk management grows.
5. Collect and assemble existing philosophical and policy statements. Review board minutes and master plans for previously adopted statements.
6. Write your philosophy and policy statement.

Step 2. Needs Assessment

Task—Take a critical look at your current risk-management practices using these 16 steps to managing risk as a guide.

Note: It would be a rare exception if you did not already have many items on the outline in place. What may be different for you is the overall systematic, step-by-step analysis of your strengths and weaknesses.

Suggested approach
1. Form a task force headed by your risk management coordinator or a key administrator to review your current situation.
2. Use the 16-step checklist (Table 1) to do a preliminary analysis of your risk-management program.
3. Determine where your strengths and weaknesses appear on the checklist.
4. Develop a work program based on weaknesses by assigning task force members to specific problem areas. Use Step 3, Goals and Objectives, for establishing reasonable time frames.

Step 3. Goals and Objectives

Task—Establish the goals and objectives that you would like to meet through your risk-management effort.

Goals tend to be rather general and open-ended; something to strive for.

Objectives are specific short-term projects that lead toward goal completion. Objectives need to be written with stated standards that the organization can use to judge the effectiveness of the program.

Table 1
Preliminary Sixteen-Step Checklist

	Presently identified		Written documentation		Need improvement		Will be completed by (___) Date	Actually completed by (___) Date
	Yes	No	Yes	No	Yes	No		
1. Philosophy/Policy								
2. Needs Assessment								
3. Goals and Objectives								
4. Site and Facility Development								
5. Program Development								
6. Supervision								
7. Establishment of Rules, Regulations, Procedures								
8. Safety Inspections and Investigations								
9. Accident Reporting and Analysis								
10. Emergency Procedures								
11. Releases, Waivers, Agreements to Participate								
12. Methods of Insuring Against Risk								
13. In-service Training								
14. Public Relations								
15. Outside Specialists, Legal/Insurance								
16. Periodic Review								

Suggested approach

1. Review current goals and objectives to determine:
    a. Which ones apply to risk management.
    b. Which ones can be adopted.
    c. Check current goals and objectives against the risk-management outline to determine deficiencies, and, where found, establish a new list of goals and objectives.
2. If goals and objectives are nonexistent, review the risk-management outline and assign teams to develop goals and objectives for specific areas of interest to them.

Sample Goal / Objective Document

Goal:

To develop a comprehensive risk-management plan that will encompass all departmental operations.

Objectives:

1. By the end of (specify month), secure policy direction from governing authority regarding the development of a risk-management plan.
2. By (specify time), appoint a risk-management coordinator.
3. Inform entire staff by (specify time) of the development of a comprehensive risk-management plan.

Here are some additional goals and objectives that your safety committee may consider:

1. The number of first-aid claims resulting from the summer recreation program will be reduced 10 percent next summer.
2. All lifeguards employed by the jurisdiction will be certified.
3. All employees will be trained in CPR.
4. All swimming pools will conform with state and federal health guidelines.
5. All indoor facilities will be inspected at least ____times annually.
6. All playgrounds will be inspected____times annually.

Note: Each part of the risk-management outline will need its own set of objectives with specific time-frames. Experience has shown that employees who help create their own goals and objectives are more apt to carry them out. It is well worth the effort to involve staff rather than impose goals and objectives on them.

Step 4. Site and Facility Development

Task—In the planning, layout, design, and construction of sites and physical facilities, it is important to work closely with architects, engineers, program specialists, landscape architects, and builders to assure:

1. Elimination of all potential site and building hazards
2. Conformance to all applicable building codes
3. Conformance to federal, state, and local rules and regulations including size, layout, health, fire, emergency, and accessibility standards
4. Functional, aesthetically pleasing facilities

Suggested approach

1. Review current site and facility development projects and make a list of desirable practices from previous developments plus a similar list of undesirable experiences to avoid.
2. Inform architects, planners, and designers of your intent to be involved as part of the team.
3. Like all professionals, architects, planners, and designers cannot work in a vacuum. Tell them what you and your staff want and what you will and will not accept. If you expect the facility to meet national and/or international competitive standards, say so up front.
4. Include your board, staff, and the public in the process. It is human nature to be supportive of something you have been involved in from the beginning.

Develop specific reporting sheets for each site and facility. Be certain to include the following types of information.

Identify facility: _____

Date of review: _____

Specific use of the facility: _____

Step 5. Program Development

Task—It is your obligation to provide consumers with quality recreation experiences, professionally taught according to acceptable standards. You have a duty to protect your governing authority, your staff, and volunteers by adhering to a program based upon the following approaches:

Suggested approach
1. Activities should be taught by qualified personnel. Instructors, including volunteers, should demonstrate certifiable qualifications. If the volunteers are not trained, it is your responsibility to require training appropriate to the task.
2. Require instructors to teach progressively in keeping with the principles of human development and in accord with the participant's skill and experience levels.
3. Provide sufficient numbers of leaders for the program, equipment, and areas used.
4. Point out potential dangers to the participants and parents. Be specific and straightforward, and require releases, waivers, or agreements to participate where necessary.
5. Keep records on file, including, but not limited to:
   a. Instructor qualifications
   b. Medical exam clearances
   c. Evaluations
   d. Safety instruction
   e. Lesson plans
   f. Eligibility requirements
   g. Schedules
   h. Manuals of operation
   i. Emergency procedures
   j. Reports for accidents, injuries, or incidents
   k. Releases/waivers
   l. Agreements to participate

6. Make certain each program has been authorized by the administration and governing authority.

It is essential that the governing authority give credence to activities, field trips, etc. in the form of a policy statement.

Sample Authorization Statements

We (name of authority) hereby authorize our staff to offer programs in

_____.

(specific programs)

or

We (name of authority) hereby authorize field trips as an integral part of our program offerings.

Step 6. Supervision

Task—Develop a plan of supervision that embraces the philosophy of managing risk you set forth in Step 1; to provide the highest level of service, using only qualified leaders and volunteers in accord with the best standard of care possible.

Suggested approach—Identify and inform the staff of the philosophy of the organization with an emphasis on the standard of care.

1. Interpret the aims, objectives, and policies of the organization.
2. Act as a liaison between staff and administrators.
3. Aid in formulating and interpreting job descriptions.
4. Assist with plans for specific programs, budgets, or facilities.
5. Evaluate the progress of staff and programs.
6. Build creative human relationships.
7. Identify activity, location, and staff-participation ratios.
8. Guide staff to attain expected accomplishments including:

a. Knowledge of self and others
b. The "why" of the program
c. The step-by-step procedure of visualizing, planning, organizing, assigning, and following through
d. Ability to encourage initiative
e. Ability to work democratically
f. Ability to observe and be sensitive
g. Ability to make decisions
h. Ability to communicate
i. Ability to act and react
j. Awareness of emergency procedures
k. Knowledge of surroundings and consciousness of participant's physical condition, fatigue, or heat exhaustion
l. Alertness to environmental changes due to weather, including snow, wind, rain, and lightning

Note: Remember, if employees, including volunteers, claim to be qualified, they should be prepared to provide a standard of care in keeping with that of a reasonable and prudent professional. If you as an administrator or supervisor are aware of incompetent employees or volunteers and choose to do nothing about it, you too could be implicated if legal action is taken against such individuals.

See appendix for supervisor's evaluation form.

Plan of Supervision—Goal: Prepare a written plan of supervision for each site, facility, and program component.

Example: Using a swimming pool as an example, a plan of supervision would include, but not be limited to:

1. Qualifications of staff
2. Documented proof of current staff qualifications
3. Written and signed job descriptions
4. Documented evaluations of performance
5. In-service training schedules, including outlines of material covered
6. Documented standards for pool capacity
7. Documented standards for ratio of lifeguards to swimmers.

8. Documented plan showing lifeguard stations, areas of supervision, rotation schedules, specific danger areas, etc.
9. Water clarity and purification standards
10. Posted emergency procedures
11. Documented proof of in-service training for emergencies
12. Written lesson plans for all skill levels
13. Safety checklists, including but not limited to specific instructions related to:
    a. Pool deck
    b. Outside grounds
    c. Change rooms
    d. Gates and fences
    e. Showers
    f. Staff room
    g. Office
    h. Diving boards
    i. Slides
    j. First aid kits
    k. Backwash schedule
    l. Emergency alarm
    m. Weather monitoring
    n. Posted rules/regulations
    o. Rescue equipment
    p. Electrical equipment
    q. Water testing
    r. Deep water
    s. Doors and windows
    t. Supervision
    u. Locked lifelines

Note: If called to testify in a liability case, there is nothing as comforting as having carefully documented proof of your supervisory techniques.

Step 7. Establishing Safety Rules, Regulations, and Procedures

Task—Assemble all the safety rules and regulations pertaining to program services and the procedures used to enforce them.

Suggested approach
1. Identify all the safety rules and regulations that should be in this file, including, but not limited to:

a. Rules and regulations that have been established for use of parks, picnic areas and shelters, community rooms, buildings, and equipment.

b. Rules for golf courses, pools, beaches, tennis facilities, ice rinks, marinas, boat usage, and other aquatic equipment.

c. Rules and regulations for use of arts and crafts facilities and equipment.

2. Review all program areas for safety rules and regulations and add to above list.

3. Establish reporting and record-keeping procedures to monitor the system; update and revise as necessary.

4. Review all signage throughout your system. A complete analysis of all signs, informational, directional, warning, and so forth, should become a regular part of the risk-management program.

5. While the above rules and regulations are aimed at the consumers of your programs, it is equally important to monitor a complete safety program for employees.

Note: While the authors recognize the importance of assuring a safe and healthful working environment for employees and the necessity to encourage employers and employees to reduce hazards in the work place, this publication is primarily aimed at managing risk for the consumer of activities.

Reference is made to the Occupational Safety and Health Act (OSHA) and NIOSH, the National Institute for Occupational Safety and Health. NIOSH was established under the OSHA, but unlike OSHA,

which is under the Department of Labor, NIOSH is in the Department of Health and Human Services. All aspects of OSHA and NIOSH plus state mandates should be integrated into the risk-management plan.

See appendix for additional information about OSHA.

Safety Rules and Regulations—Identify in a general way all the facilities, areas, programs, and equipment for which you have established rules, regulations, and procedures. These include:

1. Parks
2. Water-related facilities
3. Recreation centers
4. Woodlands
5. Golf courses
6. Trails
7. Playgrounds
8. Camps

Take each general area and identify specific rules and regulations for that facility and/or program. For example: water-related facilities.

Facilities	Programs
Pools—indoor/outdoor	Swimming lessons
Beaches	Lifeguard training
Lakes	Swim teams
Ponds	General open Swimming
Rivers	Scuba lessons
Streams	Boating
Waterfalls	Scuba lessons
Canals	Wind surfing
Canoeing	

Caveat: Rules and regulations are only as good as your enforcement procedures. If rules and regulations are advertised and not enforced, it could be interpreted as a breach of duty (nonfeasance or misfeasance) on the part of the managing authority and its employees.

Step 8. Safety Inspections and Investigations

Task—Develop a routine, systematic method for safety inspections and investigations.

Suggested approach

1. Determine what is to be inspected and how frequently. Remember, it is your duty to inspect and maintain.
2. Regularity is essential. Conditions change quickly and details are soon forgotten.
3. Establish a regular pattern of inspections and demand that it be kept.
4. Develop a series of checklists suitable for easy application throughout the system.

Example: a playground equipment checklist can be made flexible enough to accommodate all similar facilities. Inspection sheets should reflect the manufacturer's recommendations for inspections plus all national, state, and local standards, if any.

5. Establish a method of reporting faulty equipment and maintenance problems that allows minimum downtime and maximum follow-up.
6. Develop a reporting and monitoring system that will allow easy access to vital statistics regarding breakdowns. "When," "where," "why," and "how often" are some of the questions needing answers.
7. Investigations will depend on the frequency and severity of damages and/or breakdowns.

Note: See appendix for sample forms.

(Hint: Carefully documented inspection schedules are evidence of reasonable care. The prudent risk manager will have duplicate copies of all safety

SAFETY INSPECTIONS INVENTORY

	On File		In Use		Needs Updating or Needs to be developed	
Title of insp. lists	yes	no	yes	no	yes	no
1. Playground equip.	___	___	___	___	___	___
2. Building insp.—int.	___	___	___	___	___	___
3. Building insp.—ext.	___	___	___	___	___	___
4. _____	___	___	___	___	___	___
5. _____	___	___	___	___	___	___
6. _____	___	___	___	___	___	___
7. _____	___	___	___	___	___	___
8. _____	___	___	___	___	___	___
9. _____	___	___	___	___	___	___

Schedule or dates for periodic inspection	Frequency of inspection
1. Playground equipment	_____
2. Building inspection—interior	_____
3. Building inspection—exterior	_____
4. _____	_____
5. _____	_____
6. _____	_____
7. _____	_____
8. _____	_____
9. _____	_____

inspections, accident reports, etc. Keep the duplicate in a location separate from the originals.)

Note: Check with your state safety board for required inspections for items such as fire equipment and elevators. Consult with your insurance broker for advice and recommendations.

Step 9. Accident Reporting and Analysis

Task—To report the facts in an objective and unbiased manner and in sufficient detail to allow for analysis and appraisal.

Suggested approach—Compare your accident report forms with the examples in the appendix.

1. The written report must be completed with extreme care, since it could be used as evidence in a suit brought against you and your governing authority.

Do not ask for or record opinions and comments about how such an accident might be prevented in the future.

2. Establish a system for recording and monitoring all accidents. You will want to know how often and where accidents occur, the severity of the accident, the time of day, and whether the activity was supervised or unsupervised. This information will allow staff to analyze frequencies and possible patterns and to make necessary adjustments in programs, equipment, or supervision.

Note: See appendix for sample accident report forms.

Step 10. Emergency Procedures

Task—Develop a procedure for handling emergencies and adapt it to all settings.

Consider the following:

1. Require first aid and CPR training for all staff, full and part-time. It is your responsibility as an employer to pay for this on-the-job training during work hours.
2. Require medical information sheets for high-risk activities, contact sports, adventure trips, and older American centers.
3. Locate first-aid kits in all department vehicles.
4. Develop a schedule for checking and restocking first-aid equipment.
5. Provide emergency procedure instruction sheets in each first-aid kit.
6. Make arrangements for emergency phone use in out-of-the-way areas.
7. Be particularly aware of emergency procedures during special events and any large gatherings. Consult with local EMTs and others providing emergency services.
8. Establish emergency evacuation plans for all facilities.
9. Provide occupational illness and injury control methods and physicals for employees.
10. Add your own particular interests and needs to this list.

Note: Emergencies can by their very nature vary from a playground accident to a sudden tornado or windstorm. They are virtually impossible to predict. It is also impossible to know how leaders and supervisors will respond under emergency conditions. The trauma normally connected with emergencies can be substantially reduced by having an emergency plan that is well documented and has become second nature for all employees through proper indoctrination and training.

Suggested approach
1. Assign a task force to review all current policies.
2. Ask for assistance from local professionals: EMTs, paramedics, hospitals, doctors, emergency squad personnel, police and fire departments, clinics, and anyone else who may be in a position to assist you in developing and/or improving your emergency program.

Step 11. Releases, Waivers, and Agreements to Participate

Task—Analyze your current program in light of the latest information available and make adjustments where necessary.

Suggested approach
1. Review your current philosophy toward the use of releases, waivers, and agreements to participate.
   a. Why do you use them?
   b. How are they being used? By whom?
   c. Where are they kept on file? For how long?
2. With the assistance of legal counsel, review all documents in current use.
   a. Is the language sufficient for your jurisdiction?
   b. Is the language explicit enough?
   c. What is the statute of limitations in your jurisdiction?
3. Check with professional colleagues for their ideas and ask them for samples of their forms.
4. Use the samples found in the appendix for ideas and share them with your legal counsel and staff.
5. Be sure to have your governing authority approve all new and/or revised policies.
6. Finally, develop, or revise your forms, including a written procedure for the use of each form. Document where each is filed and the location of the permanent record file.

Note: Cross-reference this section to the Negligence Chapter, under Waivers, Releases, and Agreements to Participate, pages 22-23, for details.

Step 12. Methods for Insuring Against Risk

Task—Identify the alternatives available for your jurisdiction and select the best combination that will allow the most cost-effective protection.

Suggested approach
1. Consult with your legal and insurance counselors. See Step 15.
2. Understand enough of the language in order to communicate effectively. The most common loss protection methods are:
   a. Avoidance. Simply do away with all park, recreation, and leisure service programs. It is just as futile to assume you can avoid liability problems by assuming a perfect world where all activities are conducted properly and all participants behave admirably.
   b. Exposure Avoidance. Totally avoid certain types of activities (i.g., skydiving, trampoline, rock climbing).
   c. Reduction. This is what this plan is all about: reduce your losses by planning, organizing, training, and controlling as many contingencies as possible.
   d. Retention. Retain the risk by being self-insured. This means that your organization bears the entire cost of judgments brought against you.
   e. Transference. Have others carry the risk: individual and family insurance, leasing, contracting, purchase insurance, surety bonds, and the use of waivers, hold harmless clauses, and agreements to participate. Assist staff in acquiring personal liability coverage, and encourage participants to carry insurance certificates.
   f. Pooling. By joining together, similar organizations, departments, and agencies can "pool" their resources for the purpose of providing coverage and related

risk-management services for property, liability, and worker's compensation exposures. For a more detailed explanation, look for Park District Risk Management Agency (PDRMA) information in the appendix.

Note: Check appendix for a checklist of insurance coverages.

Step 13. In-Service Training

Task—Develop a comprehensive program of in-service training for the entire staff, including members of the governing authority and volunteers.

Suggested approach

1. Identify within the organization those to be trained. For example:
   a. Board/commission or corporate members
   b. Administrators
   c. Supervisors
   d. Program leaders
   e. Volunteers
   f. Foreman
   g. Laborers
   h. Office personnel
2. Develop as many training groups as necessary to accommodate your operation. Look for commonalities of interest and work assignment among the groups.
3. Develop goals and objectives with the help of your task force for training each group identified above.

Sample In-service Training Procedure

Audience: Board/commission and/or corporate members.

Goal: To have each board/commission and/or corporate member knowledgeable of all major aspects of the system.

Objectives: Within the first three months of their term, acquaint each new board member with the following:
1. Legal provisions, authority to operate, provisions of governing statutes, or corporate by-laws.
2. Department policy statements, objectives, and history.
3. Board duties, responsibilities, and authority.
4. Powers and duties of chief executive.
5. Organizational structure.
6. Personnel policies and practices.
7. List of staff names and positions.
8. List of facilities, including size, type, location, etc.
9. Provisions governing finances, planning, programs, and public relations.
10. Procedure for managing risk within the organization.

Suggestion: Prepare a personal notebook for each member of the board that contains information about the above items. Keep it current. Some board members will want to keep it with them and others expect to have it available during board meetings.

Step 14. Public Relations

Task—In this context, public relations means working within the entire system to get the word out about your proactive philosophy of managing risk and identifying your method of follow-up on all risk-related activities.

Suggested approach.

1. Your risk-management plan, when adopted, will provide a practical and philosophical base for building a solid public relations program.

2. The fact that you have adopted a proactive approach to managing risk will begin to show up in program brochures, news releases, audio/visual presentations, speeches, staff meetings, and in-service training programs, wherever your department is discussed.

3. Public relations means

   a. Having informed, visible staff

   b. Being nice to people

   c. Consistency of rule enforcement

   d. Treating users like family

   e. Well-kept and maintained areas and facilities

   f. Using waivers, releases, and agreements to participate

   g. Employing only qualified personnel

4. There is no substitute for showing genuine concern for an injured party after the accident. A good public relations program and follow-up can often resolve bitter and unhappy feelings that may lead to unnecessary litigation. This approach, recommended by the authors, *is a good way of offering compassion without admitting fault.*

5. There are, however, differences of philosophy on what department personnel should do fol-

lowing an accident. Should you visit or call on the injured party expressing concern and best wishes, or do you ignore all contact and follow-up to avoid possible self-incrimination? Discuss this with your legal counsel and insurance underwriter, determine a plan, and administer it consistently.

Step 15. Outside Specialists—Legal/Insurance

Task—Contact and have available competent legal and insurance counselors.

Suggested approach

1. It is not unusual for public agencies either to have their own legal counsel, usually on a retainer basis, or to have access to such counsel through the city/county/state legal department. Whatever method is available to you, it is very important to be on a first-name basis with those professionals you depend on for legal counsel.

2. For private, semi-private, or commercial agencies or corporations, it is just as critical to have access to appropriate legal counsel—someone you can depend on for competent advice and service when needed.

3. The same suggestions hold for insurance counselors. There is no substitute for good advice when it comes to using professional insurance counselors. They can and should take the guesswork out of helping you plan your insurance needs.

Note: See appendix for additional sources of information.

Step 16. Periodic Review

Task—Establish review procedures, a timetable, and have documented evidence that verifies your good intentions.

Suggested approach

1. Consider various parts of this plan from the viewpoint of frequency of review. Certain

areas will obviously stand out. For example, insurance by its very nature must be reviewed frequently. Other areas, such as safety inspections and investigations, accident reporting and analysis, emergency procedures, releases, waivers, and agreements to participate can be put on a regular schedule of review.

2. Use the first 15 steps of this plan as a checklist to make certain you are touching all the bases.

3. Be able to show evidence that you do, in fact, take your obligation to manage risk very seriously.

Special Note: *This book is not designed to render legal advice or legal opinion. Such advice may only be given by a licensed, practicing attorney, and only when related to actual fact situations. This warning is particularly pertinent because of the nature of the topics covered herein; these cases and negligence law are largely controlled by individual state law, and such matters should always be checked with the department, agency, organization, or private company counsel.*

C h a p t e r

6

Security and Personal Safety

KEYWORDS

Social threats

Electronic monitoring

Gangs

Law enforcement

Vandalism

Bullies

Warning devices

Weather-related threats

Crime scene

Natural predators

The purpose of this chapter is to create an awareness of potential security and personal safety issues confronting park, recreation and leisure service agencies. Following this chapter you should be able to:

1. *Comprehend the magnitude of security and personal safety issues that park, recreation, and leisure service agency personnel face in a changing society*
2. *Learn how to protect yourself, your agency and your staff from harm, lawsuits and a variety of safety issues*
3. *Be informed about the dangers inherent in bullying, gangs, and other anti-social activities*
4. *Actions that may be taken to reduce threats from crimes and terrorism*
5. *Understand the purpose and place of law enforcement in your agency*

In the early spring and late fall, campground managers can attest to the fact that retirees in RVs will tend to cluster together in an otherwise empty campground. They do this for two reasons: to facilitate social interaction and provide a sense of security in numbers. Through well-accepted and extensive behavioral research, psychologist A. H. Maslow determined that along with food and shelter, security and personal safety were basic needs of human existence. (*A Theory of Human Motivation*, A. H. Maslow, 1943)

When people feel that they are not safe in their activities, they will seek locations where they feel it is safe or they will provide for their own safety by securing locks, installing iron bars, obtaining firearms, installing alarms, or other devices that enable them to live in a relatively safe environment. Iron bars on windows, multiple locks on doors, alarm systems, and ready firearms are indications that people are worried about their personal safety. Joining gangs, while counterproductive, is a method by which young

people find some safety from harassment and social isolation.

Security measures taken by organizations should meet the needs of specific activities and groups. Individuals can feel threatened by international terrorists or be terrorized by playground bullies. It makes little difference where the terror comes from; fear of bodily harm or threatening behavior diminishes or destroys the pleasure of leisure activities. Recreation and leisure providers must provide a setting that is safe if they want to be successful and serve their public.

THREATENING ACTIVITIES

There are a number of activities that are easily identified as threatening; however, threats can be either real or perceived. Wise park, recreation, and leisure managers should attempt to respond to all categories of threats in some manner to the public.

Some perceived threats can be handled with a reassuring telephone call.

Weather-Related Threats

Adults understand threats to their well-being in the context of their own experience and their own knowledge of the environment. Natural environment threats may be related to weather factors. Those involved in recreation and other leisure activities may be concerned that their activity will be disrupted because of weather-related events. They may also fear for their personal safety in severe weather events. Tornadoes, hurricanes, flooding, lightning, and extreme temperatures have always created concern. Most people check the weather prior to engaging in outdoor activities, yet extreme conditions such as tornadoes and lightning are known to develop in a relatively short period of time. A sudden strong wind while sailing can cause high waves and dangerous conditions.

Managers should recognize their responsibility to warn participants and guests of weather conditions that threaten their safety. Weather warnings related to flooding and hurricanes normally are given a number of hours in advance of the event. Extreme temperature changes can jeopardize the safety of those who are new to the environment. As an example, a person visiting a very hot Denver, Colorado in the summer may wish to visit Rocky Mountain National Park. The differences in elevation can result in conditions that will result in hypothermia when the individual is exposed to the nighttime air at the higher elevation of Rocky Mountain National Park. Daytime temperatures in Denver can be more than 100 degrees Fahrenheit while the temperature can drop below freezing at Rocky Mountain National Park during the summer.

Possible Actions That Can Be Taken in Weather-Related Threats

Warning devices providing sound or visual warning such as signaling flags, sirens, and flashing lights should be in place in areas that have a history of extreme weather events. Organizations should use mass news media outlets to broadcast warnings. On-site signing and warnings on maps and brochures should inform visitors of the possibility of hypothermia, flash flooding, and high tides. Non-local visitors may not be knowledgeable of the local weather conditions.

Threats From Plants and Animals

One of the most enjoyable aspects of outdoor activities is the chance to see wildlife in its natural environment. Watching wildlife and eco-tourism are ever-increasing leisure activities enjoyed by the public. On the other hand, wildlife can present a significant danger to the public and under certain circumstances a great amount of fear in humans. In interactions between humans and wildlife, humans can be naive about the dangers inherent in wildlife contact.

The thought of swimming with a shark or alligator nearby is nightmarish for most. Foolish acts by individuals when viewing large animals commonly result in numerous injuries and some deaths each year. There are a significant number of injuries and deaths each year in Yellowstone National Park resulting from people trying to get too close to wildlife, particularly bison. Natural predators such as grizzly bears, sharks, and cougars cannot distinguish humans from any other prey. Humans have a natural fear of snakes and avoid them, yet many do not appreciate the inherent dangers related to all wildlife.

Domestic animals can also threaten recreationists. Most children fear aggressive neighborhood dogs. Family pets bite hundreds of people each day. Some domestic livestock can be aggressive under certain circumstances and can injure or kill humans. Household pets, especially when they form packs, have been known to attack humans. They may be docile companions with their own families, but become aggressive and wild when allowed to run free.

Many people fear insects that carry diseases such as hepatitis, malaria, Rocky Mountain spotted fever, West Nile Disease and Lyme disease. Insects and animals can transmit diseases to humans. Some people are particularly susceptible to wasp and hornet stings. Mosquitoes and ants can result in untold misery for the outdoor visitor.

Visitors have a miserable time when they come into contact with plants such as poison ivy, poison oak, thistle, cactus, and other toxic or thorned vegetation. Many plants are poisonous when ingested.

Possible Actions That Can Be Taken in Areas Where Plants and Animals Pose a Threat

Participants exposed to animals must be warned about the dangers involved. As an example, campers must be warned about the storage of food in areas frequented by bears. Warnings must be given to recreationists when they are exposed to animals that are known to attack humans. Some plants and animals create common nuisance problems; however, most people are unaccustomed to living in an outdoor environment. They do not appreciate the dangers involved with disease-carrying insects, poisonous plants, and most wild animals. Warning visitors of potential dangers is important in protecting public interest. Warnings can be issued by signs, be part of area maps and brochures, or be disseminated through mass media.

Societal Threats

While nature provides some threats to the leisure participant, a major proportion of human concern originates from their contacts with other human beings. Humans constantly think about their personal susceptibility to crime and most recently, their exposure to both domestic and international terrorism. Society appears to have a fascination with crime exemplified by the popularity of television programs featuring crime and law dramas and real-life police pursuits. People definitely know they are subject to danger from other humans.

The park, recreation, and leisure field is as susceptible to crime and terrorism as any other facet of our society. Youth gangs terrorize and vandalize neighborhoods that include parks. Gangs mark park properties as part of their "territory." Intruders from other gangs and even casual visitors can be subject to violent acts when visiting a "gang-owned" park. Drug dealing, mugging, rape, and robbery may be common events in the "gang-owned" parks. In some cities gangs take possession of the parks at night and the local residents utilize the park during the day. Even when gangs are not present in parks, individual criminals may prey upon park users by robbing and assaulting park visitors. Violent acts or the anticipation of such acts, discourage people from using parks or attending events that subject them to personal harm.

Some recreation and leisure events attract large numbers of people. The bombings of women's clinics, the 1996 Olympics bombing at a downtown Atlanta park, and the bombing of Murrah Federal Building in Oklahoma City represent acts by domestic terrorists. These acts by extreme political activists, malcontents, the mentally ill, and those looking for notoriety are best described as acts of domestic terrorism. International terrorist acts such as the September 11, 2001, attack on New York City's Twin Towers may discourage public participation in large sports gatherings, festivals, leisure travel, and other activities where large numbers of people gather.

As a result of the September 11 attack, most people welcome thorough security at major events. Terrorists are not selective. They do not care if adults or children are targeted. They care only about the maximum number of casualties and the greatest psychological damage they can cause by their actions.

Possible Actions That Can Be Taken to Reduce Threats from Crime and Terrorism

A visible and active police presence reduces crime and terrorist acts. Electronic surveillance identifies threatening activities. Urban parks should be designed to allow passing police and the general public to see into and through the park. Designs and landscaping that allow park users to be unobserved invite crime and fear. In areas where graffiti is common, facility designs that reduce vertical surfaces can reduce "tagging." Effective lighting reduces nighttime crime. Terrorist acts may be the most difficult to plan an effective defense against. When we plan to protect the public from terrorists there is a side benefit that the presence of police officers and security personnel will also protect the public from the activities of criminals engaged in selling drugs, robbery, bullying, and other illegal acts.

When recreation, park, and leisure providers anticipate a gathering of large numbers of people in a single location, or sponsor well-known speakers or guests, managers should coordinate their security efforts with local or federal law enforcement officers. Security gates may be needed where people can be searched for drugs, alcohol, explosives, firearms, or other dangerous weapons. Isolated parks can be monitored through cooperative agreements with other nearby law enforcement agencies or through electronic monitoring. Effectively fenced, gated, and locked properties significantly reduce crime only when they are monitored or patrolled by law enforcement personnel. Children should have a park and recreation experience free of fear. Society demands that managers make a special effort to ensure that children are safe. Yet, there are predators, drug dealers, bullies, and terrorists who prey upon those less likely to resist (children) in our communities. Park and recreation settings may present a setting where they who would do harm to children may find their prey.

Hiring new "safe" employees presents a well-defined problem for organizations and agencies. Most that we hire are honest and ethical, yet when it comes to children, special precautions are necessary to protect their interests. Child predators will seek out employment in organizations who have children in programs and activities. Agencies and organizations should request a copy of the criminal history or release of juvenile records of those whom they anticipate will be hired, either seasonally or permanently. Please note that anyone using criminal history information for a purpose not authorized may be subject to criminal prosecution. (See appendix for examples of criminal history request forms.)

Both international and domestic terrorists appear to find no remorse in the death of children. Playground bullies create terror in children. Children will not use facilities or participate in activities frequented by bullies. Bullies affect both the mental and physical well-being of children in a significant way.

Bullying

Why address bullying in a book about risk management for park, recreation and leisure services? Very simply, bullying provides a significant risk for those who fall victim to this sometimes ignored activity. Each year many children and adults are injured and maimed in our public parks and leisure service agencies as a direct result of bullying. The mental/psychological damage may be much more damaging than the physical damage. An awareness of this insidious hazard should be a priority in the selection and training of park and recreation personnel.

All of us, at one time or another, have experienced bullying in one of its more degrading ways. We have either bullied or been bullied or been witness to bullying. Bullying is most often associated with schools and most generally with playgrounds. So much so that schools across the country are beginning to eliminate recess as part of school activities. Not only is this an indictment of school personnel and their inability to cope with bullying, it is another blow to the fitness of children. Eliminate recess and we contribute to the already-sad state of affairs regarding child obesity, the early onset of diabetes and other childhood illnesses that will stay with them the rest of their lives. While our emphasis here is on children, there are many ways that teens and adults bully one another. The many faces of bullying include taunting, verbal abuse, written communications, shoving, intimidation, exclusion from teams, societies, and pure physical abuse such as "swirling" and "hazing" all designed to embarrass and degrade. Then too, who can forget the recent shootings and stabbings by "extreme bullies" who bring firearms and other lethal weapons to schools and playgrounds.

For years we have dismissed bullying by saying, "Oh, it's just in fun, they don't mean anything by it"; or "It's a right of passage, it happens to everyone"; or "It is just part of growing up". It is one thing to be the bully and quite another to be the recipient of nasty, hurtful, and degrading behavior.

As we suggest in Chapter Five, in a discussion about establishing policies, it may be prudent for the park and recreation board, or agency board, to adopt a policy relating to bullying. For example, the State of Indiana requires all school systems in the state to define bullying and adopt a policy for disciplinary action. One such definition defines bullying as: *"Overt, repeated acts or gestures involving verbal or written communications transmitted, physical acts committed or any other behavior committed by a student or groups of students with the intent to harass, ridicule, humiliate or harm another student. Students responsible for bullying will be subject to disciplinary action."*

When park and recreation and agency board members establish a policy related to bullying, they are making a statement saying that bullying will not be tolerated in their programs, thus giving staff direction and authority to carry out disciplinary action for those who offend others by bullying.

A recent Secret Service analysis of school shooting cases found that two-thirds were acts of revenge for being bullied, says University Professor Russell Skiba, lead author of *Preventing Bullying and Harassing*, a University Of Iowa Department of Education Support Manual. Professor Skiba notes that prevention programs are among the most effective ways to curtail bullying. He says that punishing after the fact does little good and that bullying is all about power, it is *not* just a rite of passage.

School systems across the country have joined together to conduct workshops and convocations describing the consequences of bullying, acknowledging the seriousness and sharing experiences on how to deal with the problems.

We strongly urge park, recreation, and leisure services agency personnel to join with their local school authorities in a full-scale attempt to understand the consequences of bullying and what each may do in their respective environments to curb this problem.

Possible Actions That Can Be Taken to Protect Children

Supervision of children by responsible adults is a positive first step to protect children. Electronic monitoring of playgrounds in some locations may be effective. Careful screening of all persons hired to work with children or those who volunteer to work with children should be done before they are allowed to supervise children. Children should know that bullies will not be tolerated and that children who do bully will be removed from the play and recreation area. Children should be invited to report bullies or other suspicious persons to their parents or to activity supervisors.

PURPOSES OF LAW ENFORCEMENT

Recreation and park administrators must first establish the purpose of law enforcement. In park management, law enforcement has three primary functions:

1. Protect the people from other people
2. Protect the park environment (property and resources) from the people
3. Protect the people from the environment

One of the primary purposes of law enforcement is to protect people from the illegal or offensive behavior of others. While protecting people from other people, the behavior is often considered criminal in nature. Should an organization fail to protect people using their facilities from the offensive behavior of other participants or guests, then the organization or agency may be subject to lawsuits. A riot at a recreation or sports event may subject the sponsoring agency to civil lawsuits.

When recreation managers come upon a crime scene, it is very important that the evidence found in the area be preserved. Efforts should be made to make certain that unauthorized individuals do not enter or destroy important evidence that is normally part of a crime scene. (See Appendix F or detailed information on preserving evidence.) People need to be protected from the facilities or environment they are using for their recreation or leisure pursuit. Whether it is a secured door or a bear warning sign in a campground, people must be protected from potential injuries resulting from the participation in activities.

Law enforcement and managers have the responsibility to protect the environment, natural and manmade, from people who through ignorance or intention, misuse facilities, land, or resources.

Depending upon the situation, managers must determine the profile of law enforcement that will best fit their operations. Managers have the following choices or combination of choices:

1. Uniformed law enforcement officers
2. Motorized pass-through patrols (cost efficient, very little contact with the users)
3. Horseback patrols (primarily for public relations and public crowd control)
4. Walking patrols (good public contact opportunity)
5. Bicycle patrols (provides mobile coverage in areas without adequate roads)
6. K-9 police teams (particularly useful in drug-related crime areas and suspect apprehension)
7. Non-uniformed law enforcement officers
8. Utilized for crime detection
9. Utilized for crime investigation (detective) purposes
10. Electronic surveillance (television, cameras, sound sensing, motion detection)

11. Identification of potential or illegal acts or problems

12. Identification of potential or illegal acts with immediate follow-up by a law enforcement response team

13. Other protective devices

14. Alarm systems that sound alarms or turn on lights. Usually used to frighten individuals entering property

15. Dogs on site that are trained to bark or attack when someone approaches the property

Good law enforcement efforts that match the needs of specific areas allow people to enjoy their recreation experience.

Endnotes/
Bibliography

Endnotes

1. *Tampa (Florida) Tribune*, August 21, 2006.
2. *Judicial Business of the United States Courts*, 2006, p. 27.
3. Administrative Office of the United States Courts, 2006 Accumulative Report.
4. *Webster's II, New Riverside University Dictionary*, Boston: Riverside Publishing Company, 1979.
5. *Black's Law Dictionary*, Fifth Edition, St. Paul, Minnesota: West Publishing Company, 1979.
6. Dolan, Edward F., Jr. (1972). *Legal Action*, Chicago: Contemporary Books, Inc.
7. Kaiser, Ronald A. (1986). *Liability and Law in Recreation, Parks, and Sport* (p.40). Englewood Cliffs, New Jersey: Prentice-Hall, Inc. Reprinted by permission.
8. 29 U.S.C.A. Paragraphs 1346, 1402, 2110, 2401, 2402, 2411, 2412, 2671-2680. See Wright, the Federal Tort Claims Act, 1957, Gottlieb, The Federal Tort Claims Act—A Statutory Interpretation.
9. 28 U.S.C.A. Section 2674.
10. 28 U.S.C.A. Section 2674. 13.
11. 28 U.S.C.A. Paragraphs 1346(b), 2674.
12. See the Federal Employees Liability Reform and Tort Compensation Act of 1988, Public Law 100-694.
13. 28 U.S.C.A. Paragraph 2680(a). See Dalehite v. United States, 1953, 346 U.S. 15; Harris v. United States, 10 Cir. 1953, 295 F.2d 765.
14. See Leflar and Kantrowitz, *Tort Liability of the States*, 1954, 29 N.Y.U.L. Rev. 1363.
15. See for example, Jenkins v. North Carolina Department of Motor Vehicles, 1956, 244 N.C. 560, 94 S.E. 2d 577. (State Tort Claims Act applies only to a "Negligent Act," not to intentional shooting.)
16. van der Smissen, Betty. (1990). *Legal Liability and Risk Management For Public and Private Entities*. (p. 179-195). Cincinnati, Ohio: Anderson Publishing Company.
17. For detailed information on all states regarding recreational user statutes refer to the publication *Recreational User Statutes: A Review of Landowner Hold-Harmless Laws in the United States*, prepared for the American Motorcyclist Association by Betty van der Smissen, J.D.
18. Gross negligence is determined when the defendant knows or should know the results of his or her acts.
19. Kozlowski, James C. (1986). Recreational Use Law Applies to Public Land in NY, NE, ID, OH, and WA. *Parks and Recreation*. (p. 22). October, 1986. Also see *Black's Law Dictionary*, Fifth Edition. (p. 32).
20. Indiana Code Annotated, Paragraph 14-2-6-3 and 4-16-3-1 to 3.
21. *57 American Jurisprudence*, Second Edition, 1971, sec. 1, p. 333, Municipal, School, and State Tort Liability.
22. *Black's Law Dictionary*. (p. 584). Fifth Edition.
23. *Webster's II, New Riverside University Dictionary* (1984). (p. 1013).
24. *Black's Law Dictionary*. (p. 584). Fifth Edition.
25. van der Smissen, Betty. (1986). *Legal Liability of Cities and Schools for Injuries in Recreation and Parks*. (p. 78-79). Cincinnati, Ohio: W.H. Anderson Company.
26. *Black's*, p. 950.
27. Id. at 962, 902, and 950.
28. Prosser, W. & Keaton, W. (1984). West Publishing Company. (p. 257).

29. Prosser, William L. (1980). *Law of Torts*. (p. 228). St. Paul, Minnesota: West Publishing Company. Also see *Palmer Brick Co. v. Chenall*, 119 Ga. 837 (1904), 47 S.E. 329.

30. Id. at p. 236.

31. *Black's Law Dictionary*. (p. 352). Fourth Edition.

32. *57 American Jurisprudence*. (p. 477). Second Edition, Section 98.

33. Id. at 447.

34. Id. at 448.

35. *Black's*, p. 113.

36. Prosser, *Law of Torts*, p. 433.

37. *Comparative Negligence*, Volume 1, Chapter 2.

38. *Black's*, p. 931.

39. van der Smissen, p. 92

40. Prosser, *Law of Torts*. (1980). (p. 427). St. Paul, Minnesota: West Publishing Company.

41. Prosser, William L. (p. 970-975). *Torts*, Fourth Edition.

42. Kaiser, Ronald A. (1986). *Liability and Law in Recreation, Parks, and Sports*. Englewood Cliffs, NJ: Prentice-Hall, Inc.

43. *McMillin Municipal Corporation*, Third Edition, Section 58.

44. *Black's Dictionary*. (p. 508). Fifth Edition, defining the words "exculpatory statement."

45. Kaiser, Ronald A. (1986). *Liability and Law in Recreation, Parks, and Sports*. Englewood Cliffs, NJ: Prentice-Hall, Inc.

46. van der Smissen, Betty. (1985, March). *National Safety Network Newsletter, 1*, (4).

47. *Black's*. (p. 1260). Fifth Edition.

48. Re-statement (Second) of Tort, Section 332.

49. Kaiser, Ronald A. (1986). *Liability and Law in Recreation, Parks, and Sports*. Englewood Cliffs, NJ: Prentice-Hall, Inc.

50. *Black's* (p. 830). Fifth Edition.

51. Mounsey v. Ellard, 363 Mass. 693, 297 N. E. 2d 43.

52. Samuel E. Pentecost Construction Company v. O'Donnel, 112 Ind. App. 47, 39 N.E. 2nd 812, 817.

53. Re-statement (Second) of Tort, Section 330.

54. *Black's*. (p. 1348). Fifth Edition.

55. Lockhart, Kamisar, and Choper, *Constitutional Law*. (1980). Fifth Edition. (p. 1164). St. Paul, Minnesota: West Publishing Company.

56. Amback v. Norwick, 441 U.S. 68 (1979), also see Sugarman v. Dougall 413 U.S. 34 (1939).

57. Dayton Board of Education v. Brinkman, 443 U.S. 526 (1979) also see Regents of the University of California v. Bakke, 438 U.S. 265 (1978).

58. Sherbert v. Verner, 374 U.S. 190 (1977).

59. Craig v. Boren, 429 U.S. 190 (1977).

60. Geduldig v. Aiello, 417 U.S. 484 (1974), *also see* United States v. Flores, 540 F. 2d 432 (9th Circuit 1976).

61. Massachusetts Board of Retirement v. Murgia 427 U.S. 618 (1969).

62. Simpson v. Reynolds Metals, Inc., 629 F 2d 1226 (1981).

63. Shapiro v. Thompson, 394 U.S. 618 (1969).

64. Pickering v. Board of Education, 391 U.S. 593 (1968).

65. NAACP v. Alabama, 357 U.S. 449 (1958).

66. Roe v. Wade 410 U.S. 113 (1973).

67. Section 706(g) of the Civil Rights Act of 1964.

68. 29 U.S.C.A. 206.

69. National Labor Relations Act, 49 Stat. 449 (1935) as amended by 61 Stat. 136 (1947), 65 Stat. 601 (1951), 72 Stat. 945 (1958)m 73 Stat. 541 (1959), 88 Stat. 395 (1974): 29 U.S.C. 151-69.

70. Public Law 90-202 Act of 1967 with Amendments. This law parallels the Civil Rights Act of 1964 with intent.

71. 29 U.S.C.A. 706, a comprehensive statute that establishes a federal program to assist handicapped individuals to assume a role in society.

72. 28 CFR 35, 36; 29 CF 1630; and 49 CFR 37, Gives civil rights protection to individuals with disabilities. It guarantees equal opportunity with disabilities in employment, public accommodations, transportation, communications, and state and local services.

73. Anderson and Kumpf, Business Law, Uniform Commercial Code, 1964, p. 228.

74. Ibid, p. 229.

75. Occupational Safety and Health Act, 29 U.S.C.A. 651 et seq.

76. Act of November 21, 1974 (P.L. 93-502, 88 Stat. 1561 as amended; 5 U.S.C. 552).

77. Also see Lockhart, Kamisar, and Choper, Constitutional Law, Fifth Edition, 1980, p. 507-525.

78. Miller, Lori K., Fielding, Lawrence, W., & Fitts, B.G., Implementation of the Performance Appraisal Process: Concerns for the Health Club Manager, *Journal of Legal Aspects of Sport*, (3)1, 1993, 44-50.

79. Dell v. Montgomery Ward, 811 F. 2d 970 (6th Cir. 1987).

80. Griggs v. Duke Power Company, 721 U.S. 430 (1971).

81. Gaines v. Cuna Mutual Insurance Society, 661 F. 2d 982 (5th Cir. 1992).

82. Wollery v. Brad, 741 F. Supp 667 (E.D. Mich, S, D, 1990).

83. Roe v. General Motors, 457 F. 2d 348 (5th Cir. 1972).

84. Loiseau v. Department of Human Resources of the State of Oregon, 567 F. Supp 1211 (District of Oregon, 1983).

85. Roe v. General Motors, 457 F. 2d 348.

Bibliography

American Society for Testing and Materials (ASTM). Publication F 1487-05. *Standard Consumer Safety Performance for Playground Equipment for Public Use.*

Appenzeller, Herb, & Thomas. (1980). *Sports and courts.* Charlottesville, VA: The Michie Company.

Appenzeller, Herb. (1987). *Physical education and the law.* Charlottesville, VA: The Michie Company.

California Department of Education website: Search for Bullying Resources.

Child Abuse and Neglect, www.childwelfare.gov.

Connors, Eugene T. (1981). *Educational tort liability and malpractice.* Bloomington, IN: Phi Delta Kappa.

Decof, Leonard, & Godosky, Richard. (1979). *Sports injury litigation.* Denver, CO: Practicing Law Institute.

Frakt, Arthur N., & Rankin, James S. (1982). *The law of parks, recreation resources, and leisure services.* Salt Lake City, UT: Brighton Publishing Company.

Grimaldi, John V., & Simonds, Rollin H. (1975). *Safety management,* (3rd Ed.). Homewood, IL: Richard D. Irwin, Inc.

Handbook for public playground safety. (1991). U.S. Consumer Product Safety Commission, Washington, D.C.

Heinich, H.W., Petersen, Dan, & Rooa, Nester. (1980). *Industrial accident prevention*. New York: McGraw-Hill Book Company.

Judd, Richard L., & Ponsell, Dwight D. (1982). *The first responder*. St. Louis, MO: C.V. Mosby Company.

Kaiser, Ronald A. (1986). *Liability and law in recreation, parks, and sports*. Englewood Cliffs, NJ: Prentice-Hall.

Kozlowski, James C. (1986). *Recreation and Parks Law Reporter Quarterly*. Ashburn, VA: National Recreation and Park Association.

Love Our Children USA. www.loveourchildrenusa.org.

Miller, Lori K., Fielding, Lawrence, W., & Pitts, B.G. (1993). Implementation of the Performance Appraisal Process: Concerns for Health Club Manager. *Journal of Legal Aspects of Sport*. 3(1), 44-50.

Nygaard, Gary, & Boone, Thomas H. (1985). *Coaches' guide to sports law*. Champaign, IL: Human Kinetics Publishers.

Nygarrd, Gary, & Boone, Thomas H. (1981). *The law for physical educators and coaches*. Salt Lake City, UT: Brighton Publishing Company.

Plaford, Gary. (2006). *Bullying and the brain: Using cognitive and emotional intelligence to help kids cope*. Roman & Littlefield Publishers Inc.

Posser, William L. (1980). *Law of torts*, (Fourth Ed.). St. Paul, MN: West Publishing Company.

Shivers, Jay S. (1986). *Recreational safety*. Cranbury, NJ: Associated University Presses, Inc.

Skiba, Russell. *Preventing bullying and harassment*. University of Iowa: Department of Education Support Manual. Use website.

Standard Consumer Safety Performance Specification for Playground Equipment for Public Use. Designation F 1487-05 ASTM Standards. 100 Barr Harbor Dr. West Conshohocken, PA.

Stern, James F., & Hendry, Earl R. (1977). *Swimming pools and the law*. Milwaukee, WI: S&H Books.

Stop Bullying Now! Information, Prevention, Tips, and Games. www.stopbullyingnow.hrsa.go.

Townley, Stephen, & Grayson, Edward. (1984). *Sponsorship of sports, arts, and leisure: Law, tax, and business relationships*. London: Sweet and Maxwell.

Valente, Paula R. (1980). *Current approaches to risk management: A directory of practices*. Washington, D.C.: International City Managers Association.

U.S. Government Federal Registery (for guidelines regarding the 1991 Disabled Americans Act), Vol. 56 Number 144, 1991.

Uniform Federal Accessibility Standards, General Services Administration, Department of Defense, Department of Housing and Urban Development, U.S. Postal Service, Federal Standards 795. April 1, 1988.

van der Smissen, Betty. (1968). *Legal liability of cities and schools for injuries in recreation and parks*. Cincinnati, OH: Anderson Publishing Company.

van der Smissen, Betty. (1990). *Legal liability and risk management for public and private entities*. Cincinnati, OH: Anderson Publishing Company.

Wasserman, Natalie, & Phelus, Dean G., (Eds.). (1985). *Risk management today: A how-to guide for local government*. Washington, D.C.: International City Managers Association.

Weistart, John C., & Lowell, Cym H. (1979). *The law of sports*. Indianapolis, IN: The Bobbs-Merrill Company, Inc.

Yasser, Ray. (1985). *Sports law*. Lanham, MD: University Press of America, Inc.

Appendices

NOTE: The authors recommend that your organization consult with your Risk Manager, Safety Officer or Legal Council before adopting any of the forms in the Appendices.
Each State or legal jurisdiction may have ordinances or statutes prohibiting the use of some forms.

The authors are extremely grateful to all the park, recreation and leisure service professionals who so graciously contributed materials for this section.

Much more material was gathered than could possibly be used in this publication. Professionals from the three cities listed below contributed items considered very pertinent to the subject matter but because of their length are not printed in this text. Please request them directly from each city.

Indy Parks, Indianapolis, Indiana   *jmatting@indygov.org*
    Risk Management Plan (19pp.)
    Accident Report Manual (18pp.)

Cleveland Metro parks, Cleveland, Ohio   *trc@clevelandmetroparks.com*
    Automated External Defibrillator Policy AED (16pp.)
    Insurance and Bonds-Standard Language for Construction (9pp.)
    Commercial General Liability Insurance (4pp.)

Saint Paul, Minnesota Division of Parks and Recreation   *bob.bierscheid@ci.stpaul.mn.us*
    Emergency Procedures and First Response Information for Hillcrest Comm. Recreation Center (22pp.)
    Background Checks for Division Volunteers Who Work With Youth and Other Vulnerable Populations (4pp.)
    Banning Participants From Facilities (3pp.)
    Procedures for Medication Administration (5pp.)

Appendix A

Policy Statements, Indemnification, Employment, and Wireless Communications

- Mission Statement
- Philosophy Statement
- Our Promise to You
- Hand Gun Policy and Procedures
- Youth Athletics Policy: Training for Coaches
- Food Safety Policy for Recreation Centers
- Administrative Policy on Safety
- Policy on Photography at Park and Recreation Events
- Indemnification Agreement
- Release, Hold-Harmless and Indemnification Agreement
- Introduction to Safety for New Employees
- Request for Adult Criminal History Information
- Request for Limited Criminal History
- Release for Background Information
- Police Department Juvenile Records Release Form
- Wireless Communications Operating Procedure

"ACCIDENT PREVENTION PROGRAM"
MISSION STATEMENT

Accident prevention and safety are a fundamental responsibility of every St. Louis County Department of parks and Recreation employee. We must work together to maintain a safe environment for ourselves and our park visitors. No job, program or event should be considered to have been effectively completed unless workers have followed every precaution to protect themselves, their fellow workers, and the public from accidental injury.

Maintaining a safe and accident free environment allows the Department to perform those functions and services that are mandated without interruption. Therefore, every employee is expected to conduct their business in a manner consistent with the safety standards and accident prevention goals that are established.

Bloomington Parks and Recreation

Risk Management Plan

I.   PHILOSOPHY STATEMENT

Responsibility for safety and risk management is an essential component of the success of the programs of the Bloomington Parks and Recreation Department. We are committed to the safety of all participants, spectators, employees and volunteers. When managing risk, the Bloomington Parks and Recreation Department has found no substitute for well-trained, capable employees and volunteers, sound safety practices and diligence in the safe operation of all programs. When all employees and volunteers within the Department are aware that risk management is valued by the staff, desired attitudes will result in performance of duties which allow the City to transfer, avoid or control risk in its recreational sports programs. Finally, it is exceptionally important that the professional staff of the Bloomington Parks and Recreation Department become personally involved in risk management, or the goal of reducing risk exposure to the Department, and to the City of Bloomington, itself, cannot be achieved.

II.   GOALS and OBJECTIVES

The risk management goals of Bloomington Parks and Recreation Department are:

A.   To provide a risk management plan which is designed to allow our participants a quality experience in a safe environment.

B.   To protect our employees and volunteers from undue risk and injury.

C.   To use ordinary and reasonable care to keep the facilities and programs reasonably safe for our visitors and participants.

D.   To properly warn participants, visitors, employees and volunteers of any hazardous or dangerous condition.

E.   To provide equipment which is safe and well-maintained for use by our participants, employees and volunteers.

F.   To provide an expedient response by our trained personnel to any accident or injury which occurs during a program activity.

G.   To provide a risk management plan which is relevant for all program areas, and is useful on a regular basis to our professional staff and employees.

SAINT PAUL PARKS AND RECREATION

Commitment Statement- *"Our Promise To You"*
The staff of Saint Paul Parks and Recreation promises to cheerfully and respectfully serve you. We will provide access to clean and safe facilities and programs with timely and effective service. We will listen and respond to your suggestions and concerns to the best of our abilities.

Mission: To sustain the lives and health of its citizens and visitors, Saint Paul Parks and Recreation will, within available resources, provide and facilitate safe, quality services, programs and facilities while preserving and enhancing natural resources and stimulating the economic vitality of the community.

Vision Statement
Saint Paul Parks and Recreation will create a comprehensive system of recreational programming, facilities and natural resource protection and enhancement that is of national quality. This system will utilize four basic principles:
- Stewardship of human and physical resources
- Innovation in programming and facility development
- Maximizing of community resources
- Facilitation and collaboration of and with community groups, agencies and businesses

These efforts will include the researching of the latest trends, the assessing of community needs and interests, the ongoing evaluation of all operations and the utilization of best practices in order to provide a healthy quality of life in our ever-changing community.

Statement of Benefits of Saint Paul Parks and Recreation:
- Fosters human development and supporting education
- Facilitates community problem solving and cooperation
- Strengthens community image and a sense of place
- Promotes economic development in Saint Paul
- Protects, sustains and revitalizes environmental resources
- Increases cultural unity and building community relationships
- Strengthens safety and security
- Provides the essential support service for park and recreational experiences

Core Functions Statement
1. Development and Operation of the Como Campus
   a. Provide for major community wide natural resource education and appreciation experiences
   b. Present unique recreation opportunities for all segments of the community
2. Development of Unique Recreational Opportunities and Protection of Natural Resources in the National Great River Park (Mississippi River Corridor)
   a. Coordinate the numerous plans that have been developed by a multitude of agencies / community organizations
   b. Carefully plan and add special recreational experiences.
3. Implementation and Maintenance of Quality Parks, Recreation and Open Spaces
   a. Allow for structured, unstructured, active and passive recreation opportunities.
   b. Ensure safety & usability of community investments
4. Development, Operation and Facilitation of Recreation, Arts and Special Events Programming and Facilities that Meet the Needs of the Community within the Established Resources
   a. Operate a system that is responsive to citizen needs, incorporates national trends and is flexible in the use of maximizing available resources.
   b. Provide facilities that serve the needs of the entire community.
5. Development and Support of Specialized Facilities and Programs that are Substantially Self-Supporting
   a. Allow for city wide participation and non-resident fee support
   b. Provide for more stable revenue source
   c. Encourage popular special events
6. Protection and Enhancement of Natural Resources
   a. Master Plan Management of Resource Areas
   b. Restoration of Degraded Areas
7. Encourage Citizen Participation
   a. Involve citizens in design and delivery of programs and facilities
   b. Encourage community collaboration and involvement
8. Develop and promote education opportunities, job preparedness and leadership development for the youth in St. Paul
   a. Second Shift Initiative
   b. Como Campus education programs, Community Education and Youth Job Corp

SAINT PAUL PARKS AND RECREATION
Policy and Procedures - RECREATION SERVICES

NUMBER: DIV. 9   **EFFECTIVE DATE:** 5-01-03

SUBJECT: Handgun Policy and Procedures

PURPOSE: To clarify how the conceal & carry law affects workers at a Parks & Recreation Facility

REQUIREMENTS (OR EXPECTATIONS)

The following information has been provided by the Saint Paul Police:

FACTS:

- This law applies only to handguns. It does not include rifles;
- The handgun does not need to be concealed;
- The permit holder may carry more than one handgun with the permit;
- The permit holder must carry the permit and a current government issued ID.   The Police will verify these items when called;
- Permit holder must be 21 years of age or older;
- Permit holder must prove they have passed the required training course;
- Permits are issued by the sheriff for the county in which the permit holder resides;
- The permit holder cannot carry while under the influence of drugs and/or alcohol.
- Permits are valid for 5 years;

WHAT STAFF SHOULD DO
Division Policy: If you see a weapon - ANY WEAPON, call 9-1-1

Remain calm, and follow these procedures...
- Do not approach the individual;
- Call 9-1-1 from a land line. This allows the call to route directly to the Saint Paul Police dispatch center. If a land line is not available, use a cell phone;
- Make the call as discreetly as possible. Go into another room or office area;
- Know the appropriate information before you place the call;
For example...
- Be prepared to provide a description of the individual carrying the handgun. Descriptions include: gender, race, age, height, weight, hair color, distinguishing features such as glasses, facial hair, jacket, cap/hat etc.
- Know the address and cross street of your facility;
- Identify yourself as City staff;
- Request the officer come into your facility and meet with you or your designated staff;
- Request the officer's name, badge number and Case Number (CN) if necessary;

Remember that the law allows a registered permit holder to
LEGALLY carry a handgun!

Saint Paul Police WILL respond to calls from City staff to verify permits.
They will: 1) Verify the permit,
2) Verify identification,
3) Respond appropriately

| SAINT PAUL PARKS AND RECREATION |
| **Policy and Procedures - RECREATION SERVICES** |

REQUIRED ITEMS AND/OR RELATED INFORMATION:

SECTION MANAGER'S RESPONSIBILITIES	SUPERVISOR'S RESPONSIBILITIES	EMPLOYEE'S RESPONSIBILITIES
Ensure all employees under his/her jurisdiction are aware of this policy and procedures.	Advise all employees of this policy and procedures.	Adhere to the policy.
Ensure that supervisors in his/her section enforce this policy and procedures.	Ensure that employees follow this policy and procedures.	Follow the procedures.
	Issue warnings or initiate disciplinary action as needed to ensure employee compliance.	Ask for additional training if needed.

Owner: Eric Thompson   **Next Review Date: 3-01-08**

YOUTH ATHLETICS POLICY: TRAINING FOR COACHES

STATEMENT
It is the position of the Division of Parks and Recreation of the city of Saint Paul that all youth coaches be trained. Coaches working with youth in the city's programs for 10U and older or any independent team not involved in the city's sponsored leagues, but practicing at a city owned facility, are required to be trained through the program offeredA program supervisor in the Recreation Services section may grant alternative certification if submitted in advance of the season.

ACCEPTABLE ALTERNATES TO ST. PAUL COACHES CERTIFICATION:
 (Written documentation of alternate certification must be submitted to and approved by a program supervisor and forwarded to the Municipal Athletics Office).
1. Current high school or college coaches certification.
2. State or national certification in the specific sport.
3. 5 year minimum coaching at the high school or junior high school level.

Note! Coaches granted a substitution for St. Paul Coaches Training are still required to abide by the expectations set for St. Paul youth coaches and sign and return the Coach's Pledge form.

IT IS THE POLICY OF THE DIVISION OF PARKS AND RECREATION OF THE CITY OF SAINT PAUL THAT;
1. All youth coaches coaching teams in city sponsored leagues and all youth coaches coaching teams in non city sponsored leagues, but use city facilities must be certified or meet the alternative qualifications.

2. Uncertified coaches, after given reasonable time to attend certification clinics or make up clinics (maximum of 30 days from the first scheduled league game), will be relieved of their coaching responsibilities until they have been certified.

3. Any team without a certified coach may not continue to participate in league play or be eligible for playoffs.

4. Coaches with non city league teams that are using city owned facilities must sign a coaches certification verification form and the form must be on file at the facility being used.

5. Non certified/alternates coaches for non city league teams will not be allowed to hold practices or games at a city owned facility.

SAINT PAUL PARKS AND RECREATION

Food Safety for Recreation Centers

Serving Snack items – such as with after school programs

- Pre-packaged food items such as: granola bars, fruit roll-ups, individually packaged chips, or snack crackers, are rarely problematic. **Guideline**: Make sure packages are not open and food items have not exceeded expiration dates on package labels.
- Dairy products, fruit juice, cheese and other similar items must be properly refrigerated at temperatures between 34 and 40 degrees. These temperatures should be checked at least daily and logged. (Similar to the guidelines for our summer lunch program) In addition, these perishable food items must be served prior to reaching their expiration dates.
- Other food items: Pre-packaged foods such as frozen pizzas, macaroni products etc. should be prepared according to manufacturer's directions and served immediately. These types of food items should be discarded if left out longer than 2 hours and should not be kept to re-serve regardless of how long they are left out.

Concession Operations

LIEP understands that recreation centers will operate concession stands during sports seasons or other special events. The following guidelines are recommended:

- Prepackaged items such as: candy, chips, soda, ice cream treats, granola bars are rarely problematic. Make sure packages are not open prior to serving and that products have not reached their expiration dates.
- With items such as hot dogs and nachos, make sure food items are cooked/heated as per package directions. Hot items should be kept hot – 160 degrees. Once items have been left out for longer than 2 hours, they should be discarded.
- Regarding cooking fresh meat – hamburgers, chicken breast, fresh brats, etc. – it is NOT recommended at our facilities. Sloppy Joe's (meat thoroughly cooked and then cooked again in the sauce) is better.

Booster Clubs

LIEP understands that Booster Clubs will host fundraisers and special events that involve serving food. All of the recommendations listed above apply, as do the following:

- Food products such as spaghettis noodles should NOT be cooked the night before and stored (even in a refrigerator) for serving the next day.
- Pre-cooked meatballs are better than us cooking our own.
- LIEP does not regulate "pot-luck" type events.

Regardless of the type of food operation, the following guidelines are for all food handlers:

- Proper hand washing is the single most important food safety practice for the food handler. Kitchens should be equipped with a separate hand washing sink, hand soap, a scrub brush and paper toweling.
- Use commercial grade pots, pans and utensils whenever possible. When replacing old food prep items, consider replacing them with commercial grade utensils.
- Wear a hat or hairnet to control hair when working around food.
- No sandals, flip-flops or other open-toed shoes when working around food, especially hot food.
- Use food handling gloves when handling food that is not wrapped or individually packaged.
- Keep hot food hot (160 degrees) and cold food cold (40 degrees).
- Thoroughly wash food preparation surfaces, knives and mixing spoons – soap and water, followed by bleach mixture clean-up, especially if preparing raw foods.
- Remove food waste and empty garbage containers immediately after an event as a routine part-of the clean-up.

CITY OF IOWA CITY

Administrative Policy on Safety

The responsibility for a healthful work environment is a shared one, resting with all individuals at every level of the City's work force. The common goal of eliminating all preventable workplace illnesses and injuries is attained through an uncompromising commitment to safety and to recognizing and controlling hazards. To this end, workers and management must work in a nonadversarial, cooperative effort to promote safety and health for all employees. Furthermore, management demonstrates its commitment by providing leadership and the necessary resources, while all employees utilize safe work practices and participate in the creation of policies that keep them from harm's way. Both recognize safety as so primary that it always takes precedence over work place shortcuts. United efforts, as well as the individual role specified below, help ensure the protection of the city's valued public servants.

Department Directors occupy a key role in the successful development of safety programs. As the highest level of management with direct contact with division heads, supervisors, and employees, they are expected to provide leadership and direction in the administration of all safety activities.

Division heads are directly responsible for maintaining all safety programs and policies. Well trained in identifying and addressing safety issues particular to their divisions, each is charged with implementing all applicable OSHA compliance programs, employee safety training, hazard assessments, accident reviews and corrective action procedures, and other injury prevention policies.

Supervisors, through their constant and cooperative efforts, account for the success of safety programs. Immediate supervisors, including lead workers and all others with supervisory responsibilities, will make certain that employees work safely and observe all safety regulations. These

2

supervisors are therefore responsible for frequent checks of equipment and working through proper division level channels to ensure the observance of safety policies.

Employees, whether permanent or temporary, are the heart of all safety efforts. Management encourages employee contributions on matters of safety. Employees are expected to follow safe work procedures and to take an active part in protecting themselves, their fellow workers, citizens, and equipment. Having first-hand knowledge of job tasks, they can detect and report to their supervisors hazardous equipment, conditions, practices, and behaviors in their work place and make corrective suggestions. Employees must observe applicable safety regulations and practices and use all safety equipment required and provided.

The Occupational Safety and Training Specialist provides service to Departments and Divisions in meeting their safety needs and acts as a City-wide safety coordinator by providing information regarding OSHA and other applicable laws, assisting with program development, recommending corrective actions, developing and providing appropriate training, and serving as a resource in all safety matters.

_____   10 -13- 97
Stephen J. Atkins, City Manager   Date

In recognition and support of this Administrative Policy on Safety as the basis for a cooperative effort by Labor and Management to provide a safe and healthful work environment for all City employees.

_____   _____
Tairi Sackfield, President   Steven Stimmel, President
AFSCME Local #183   IAFF Local #610

_____
Daniel Dreckman, President
Police Labor Relations Organization
of Iowa City

CITY OF SAINT PAUL
DIVISION OF PARKS AND RECREATION
300 City Hall Annex - 25 W. 4th Street
Saint Paul, MN 55102
(651)266-6400 - TTY (651)266-6378

Photography at Saint Paul Parks and Recreation Events

In order to provide our customers with the safest possible parks experience, the Saint Paul Parks and Recreation Division prohibits photography and recording in Park and Recreation facilities without prior permission from both the acting facility supervisor and from the subjects of the photography or recording.

Those who plan to photograph at a Saint Paul Parks and Recreation Facility

Please check with the acting facility supervisor. You must have:

1. Prior approval (verbal or written) from both the facility supervisor and the adult subject(s) of your work, and

2. Prior written approval (release form) from the legal guardian of any child whose image you wish to record.

Those not following this policy may be asked to put away their equipment or leave the facility.

Thank you for your consideration.

SAMPLE

INDEMNIFICATION AGREEMENT

The Park/Forest Preserve District or SRA shall indemnify and hold harmless the _____(Agency)_____, its officers, employees, volunteers and agents against any claims, demands, cost and expenses, including reasonable attorney's fees for the defense thereof, arising from or in connection with the District/SRA's use of _____(Agency)_____ property provided that said claims, demands, costs and expenses have not been caused by the negligence of _____(Agency)_____, its officers, employees, volunteers and agents.

The _____(Agency)_____ shall indemnify and hold harmless the Park/ Forest Preserve District or SRA, its officers, employees, volunteers and agents against any claims, demands, cost and expenses, including reasonable attorney's fees for the defense thereof, arising from or in connection with the _____(Agency's)_____use of District/SRA property provided that said claims, demands, costs and expenses have not been caused by the negligence of the District/SRA, its officers, employees, volunteers and agents.

RELEASE, HOLD-HARMLESS AND INDEMNIFICATION AGREEMENT

In consideration for permission for my child to ride along in a CITY OF BLOOMINGTON vehicle, for my child's benefit only, I agree to the following:

1.   To release, hold harmless and indemnify the City of Bloomington, its employees, officers, and agents, for any claim or claims which might arise out of any incident connected with or in any way related to riding in a City of Bloomington vehicle. This includes claims for personal injury, property damage, and/or other types of harm or injury.

2.   To release, hold harmless and indemnify the City of Bloomington, its employees, officers, and agents, for any claim or claims arising out of any incident connected with or in any way related to riding in a City of Bloomington vehicle which may be made or asserted by any other person(s) against the City of Bloomington. This includes claims for personal injury, property damage, Workers Compensation and/or any other type of harm or injury.

I understand this release binds my child, myself, my spouse, and all heirs, executors and administrators of those individuals. I have read this release and understand all of its terms. I sign it voluntarily and with full knowledge of its significance.

Purpose of Ride-Along:_____

_____   _____
Parent's signature   Date

_____   _____
Parent's name, printed   Telephone number

_____
Child's name

**Columbus Parks and Recreation Department
Introduction to Safety for New Employees**

This written introduction to safety is to be given to new employees by their supervisors before they begin their work assignments. Its purpose is to stress from the beginning the importance of safety within the parks and recreation department.

Each new employee is required to go through a general safety training covering a number of safety concerns, including blood borne pathogens. In addition, each employee must attend training on sexual harassment. This introduction does not take the place of such training. Rather, it places the employee on notice that such training is forthcoming and that the new employee must be aware of working safely.

As an employee of the Columbus Parks and Recreation Department, I will:

- Always ask the proper methods before performing any new task.
- Wear appropriate clothing and shoes, as required by my job.
- Wear all personal protective equipment required by my job.
- Lift properly, using my legs and not my back.
- Never operate any vehicles, equipment, or power machines unless I have been authorized and trained to do so.
- Immediately report unsafe work practices or safety hazards to my supervisor.
- Never be under the influence of drugs or alcohol while on duty or while on park department or City premises.
- Never take part in horseplay.
- Never perform any unsafe practice that will place myself or others in danger.
- Immediately report any accident or illness to my supervisor.
- Understand that PromptMed is the City's provider of medical services for injuries or illnesses received on the job, and should be used if medical treatment is required.
- Never touch blood or other human bodily fluids without first protecting myself with latex gloves and other protection as needed.
- Immediately report any exposure to human blood to my supervisor.
- Know and obey the safety rules in my department.
- Understand that I am most responsible for my own personal safety.
- Understand that the City of Columbus has a zero tolerance toward sexual harassment and that employees are encouraged to report incidents of sexual harassment to their supervisor, department head, or City personnel director.

Any infraction of the above rules will result in appropriate disciplinary action. Such action will take the form of verbal or written warnings, suspension, or dismissal, depending on the seriousness of the infraction.

Employee's Statement

I have read the above safety rules with my supervisor. I understand them and will apply them at all times while I am employed by the Columbus Parks and Recreation Department.

_____   _____
Printed Name of Employee   Signature of Employee

Witnessed by:

_____   _____
Supervisor   Date

REQUEST FOR ADULT

CRIMINAL HISTORY INFORMATION

ID Billing Number
00000083

(Please type or print all information)

SUBJECT of Request:

Last Name	First Name	M.I.

Date of Birth	Sex	Race

(X) Requesting AGENCY:
- or -
( ) Requesting INDIVIDUAL:

Bloomington Parks & Recreation
Name

PO Box 848   Bloomington, IN 47402
Mailing Address where this response will be sent – if mailed

Daytime Phone: 812-349-3710

LIMITED CRIMINAL HISTORY INFORMATION

REASON FOR REQUEST

> **$7.00   Mark an (X) in one box below for this request**
> Certified Check or Money Order if request is mailed
> Cash will be accepted only if request is in person

*   ( ) Has applied for a limited criminal history on himself/herself.
1.   ( ) Has applied for employment with a non-criminal justice organization or individual.
2.   ( ) Has applied for a license and criminal history data as required by law to be provided in connection with the license.
3.   ( ) Is a candidate for public office or a public official.
4.   ( ) Is in the process of being apprehended by a law enforcement agency.
5.   ( ) Is placed under arrest for the alleged commission of a crime.
6.   ( ) Has charged that his rights have been abused repeatedly by criminal justice agencies.
7.   ( ) Is the subject of judicial decision or determination with respect to the setting of bond, plea bargaining, sentencing, or probation.
8.   (X) Has volunteered services that involve contact with, care of, or supervision over a child who is being placed, matched, or monitored by a social services agency or a not-for-profit corporation.
9.   ( ) Is being investigated for welfare fraud by an investigator of the division of family and children or a county office of family and children.
10. ( ) Is being sought by the parent locator service of the child support bureau of the division of family and children: or
11. ( ) Has been convicted of any of the following:
    (A) Rape (IC 35-42-4-1) or , Criminal deviate conduct (IC 35-42-4-2), if the victim is less than eighteen (18) years of age.
    (B) Child molesting (IC 35-42-4-3).
    (C) Child exploitation (IC 35-42-4-4 (b)).
    (D) Possession of child pornography (IC 35-42-4-4 (c)).
    (E) Vicarious sexual gratification (IC 35-42-4-5).
    (F) Child solicitation (IC 35-42-4-6).
    (G) Child seduction (IC 35-42-4-7).
    (H) Incest (IC 35-46-1-3), if the victim is less than eighteen (18) years of age.

(NO-FEE AND FULL CRIMINAL HISTORY REQUEST CONTINUED ON BACK)

NO FEE   Mark an (X) in one box below for this request

NON-PROFIT ORGANIZATIONS and SCHOOL VOLUNTEERS   IC 5-2-5-13

A. ( ) Prospective adult volunteer for children (Copy of non-profit status enclosed).
B. ( ) Home Health Agency (Copy of license has been issued and on file with ISP).
C. ( ) Department of Public Welfare Day Care/Foster Home Licensing or licensee.
D. ( ) Adult volunteer for a school corporation or non-public school.

$10.00 (   ) Mark an (X) here for this request

FULL CRIMINAL HISTORY

Any individual requesting a full criminal history on themselves only, may obtain the information two (2) different ways:

1. Come into our office (address below)
    a.) Must have picture ID, or Social Security card & Birth Certificate.
    b.) $10.00 cash or money order.

2. Request by mail – please submit the following:
    a.) This form, or a simple letter requesting "full criminal history information"
    b.) A complete set of fingerprints taken by a law enforcement agency
    c.) $10.00 certified check or money order to State of Indiana (No Personal Checks)

WARNING - PENALTY FOR MISUSE

A non-criminal justice organization or individual receiving a limited criminal history may not utilize it for purposes other than those stated in the request or which deny the subject any civil right to which the subject is entitled.   IC 5-2-5-5: Any person who uses limited criminal history for any purpose not specified in the request commits a Class A misdemeanor offense.

I affirm, under penalty of perjury, that the Limited Criminal History Information requested will be used as specified.

_____   _____
          Signature of Requester   **Date**

Cash will be accepted only if request is in person: otherwise, all checks payable to **STATE OF INDIANA**

Mail request to:

Indiana State Police, Central Repository
100 North Senate Avenue, Room N302
Indianapolis, Indiana 46204-2259

BLOOMINGTON POLICE DEPARTMENT
REQUEST FOR LIMITED CRIMINAL HISTORY

I, _____, an employee of **Bloomington Parks & Recreation**
     last name, first name, MI   name of business or agency, address, phone

in the position of ___**Special Services Coordinator**_____, request a limited criminal history

(release – inspection) of _____, ____, ____, _____, _____,
                                          name   race   sex   D.O.B.   S.S.N.

who lives at _____.
                                          address

I request this information in compliance with Indiana Code 5-2-5-5:

Sec. 5. (a) Except as provided in subsection (b), on request, law enforcement agencies shall release or allow inspection of a limited criminal history to noncriminal justice organizations or individuals only if the subject of the request:
(1) has applied for employment with a noncriminal justice organization or individual;
(2) has applied for a license and criminal history data as required by law to be provided in connection with the license;
(3) is a candidate for public office or a public official;
(4) is in the process of being apprehended by a law enforcement agency;
(5) is placed under arrest for the alleged commission of a crime;
(6) has charged that his rights have been abused repeatedly by criminal justice agencies;
(7) is the subject of judicial decision or determination with respect to the setting of bond, plea bargaining, sentencing, or probation;
(8) has volunteered services that involve contact with, care of, or supervision over a child who is being placed, matched, or monitored by a social services agency or a nonprofit corporation;
(9) has volunteered services at a public school (as defined in IC 20-10.1- 1-2) or non-public school (as defined in IC 20-10.1-1-3) that involve contact with, care of, or supervision over a student enrolled in the school;
(10) is being investigated for welfare fraud by an investigator of the division of family and children or a county office of family and children;
(11) is being sought by the parent locator service of the child support bureau of the division of family and children; or
(12) has been convicted of any of the following:
(A) Rape (IC 35-42-4-1), if the victim is less than eighteen (18) years of age.
(B) Criminal deviate conduct (IC 35-42-4-2), if the victim is less than eighteen (18) years of age.
(C) Child molesting (IC 35-42-4-3).
(D) Child exploitation (IC 35-42-4-4(b)).
(E) Possession of child pornography (IC 35-42-4-4(c)).
(F) Vicarious sexual gratification (IC 35-42-4-5).
(G) Child solicitation (IC 35-42-4-6).
(H) Child seduction (IC 35-42-4-7).
(I) Incest (IC 35-46-1-3), if the victim is less than eighteen (18) years of age.

I request this information because ___**the above mentioned will be volunteering within our**___

___**department.**_____.

I understand that any person who uses a limited criminal history for any purpose not specified under I.C. 5-2-5-5 commits a class A misdemeanor. I understand that use of a limited criminal history may be unlawful under Federal Law. I understand that the use of a limited criminal history may subject me to criminal and/or civil liability. I have been advised by the Bloomington Police Department to obtain legal counsel prior to receiving any criminal history data.

_____   _____
            Date   Signature

Subscribed and sworn before me this _____ day of _____, 20___.   *Notary Seal*

                                                    _____
                                                    Signature of Notary Public

My commission expires _____ City _____ County _____

_____

Based on the information you provided: Your request is denied:

(   )   See Reverse Side   (   )   Inadequate information for identification
(   )   The Bloomington Police Dept. does not have a (   )   Reason for request does not comply with I.C.5-2-5-5
         criminal history on the individual you requested   Other_____
                                                            _____

_____ _____   _____ _____
   Records Clerk Signature   *Date*   *Records Div. Supervisor*   *Date*

RELEASE FOR BACKGROUND INFORMATION

Please read the following statement carefully before signing below:

I hereby authorize and give my consent to the release of any and all background information and/or records about me, by any person, business, agency or other entity in possession of the same, to the City of Bloomington Parks and Recreation Department, for the purpose of conducting a background check and a criminal history check. I authorize the City of Bloomington to make photocopies of this document, and such copies shall suffice in place of the original to notify persons or other entities in possession of information about me that I have freely and voluntarily agreed and consented to the matters herein.

I certify that the information contained in my volunteer application is true. I realize that misrepresentation of facts is cause for rejection of my application or dismissal from the Parks and Recreation volunteer program after acceptance. I understand that my acceptance as a Parks and Recreation Volunteer is contingent in part upon the verification that I do not have any disqualifying information on my criminal history record.

I hereby waive, release and surrender any and all rights to claims which I may have against the City of Bloomington or any of its officers, employees or agents as a result of the release of my records.

_____   _____

Signature of Applicant   Date

To be completed by Notary Public: (Bloomington Parks and Recreation Section)

Subscribed and Sworn before me, a Notary Public, this _____day of _____ , _____

My commission expires: _____

_____   Notary Public
                                                                      Printed Name: _____
                                                                      Residing in _____ County

Return to Special Services Coordinator

88

BLOOMINGTON POLICE DEPARTMENT
JUVENILE RECORDS RELEASE FORM

I, _____ , the legal parent/guardian of the below listed subject, do hereby authorize the release of criminal history information on my child for the purpose of employment.

Name of Juvenile   _____

Date of Birth   _____

Social Security No.   _____

Address: _____

Parent/Guardian Signature: _____

Date: _____

Subscribed and sworn before me this _____ day of _____, 19____.

_____
Notary Public

My commission expires_____
County of _____   _____
                                    Printed

WIRELESS COMMUNICATION
OPERATING PROCEDURE

Purpose:

The purpose of the Operating Procedure is to establish policy concerning departmental issued wireless communication equipment.

General:

The department provides wireless communication equipment to conduct departmental business when other communications means are not available. Personal cellular calls are not permitted on County issued equipment unless the employee chooses to purchase an alternate service plan. Personal numeric and text paging are allowed.

There are two types of Nextel phone devices in service. A cell phone with a two-way radio (i85s) and a two-way radio (i550). Authorized employees of the St. Louis County Department of Parks and Recreation are to follow the guidelines below in the use of Nextel equipment.

Responsibilities:

1. All equipment and accessories are the property of St. Louis County Department of Parks and Recreation. Nextel equipment is assigned to the individual except for units assigned to vehicles i.e.: crane and snow plow trucks. New employees must contact the Information Technology Supervisor in order to receive appropriate training and equipment. At that time, employees will also receive a copy of the policy and will sign an equipment voucher.

2. Should the wireless communication equipment malfunction or need repair, it should be reported immediately to the IT Section. Employees are not to go directly to a wireless communication equipment dealer for repairs or problems

3. The employee is responsible for the care and custody of this equipment and any or all damages, including theft, which occurs through negligence or neglect. Such damage or loss will result in reimbursement to the department.

4. It is the employee's responsibility to return all equipment in good operating condition to the department upon resignation or termination.

5. Supervisors will review and validate usage statements.

WIRELESS COMMUNICATION OPERATING PROCEDURE
PAGE 2

6.   When paging someone in the Department, be sure to use the numbers indicated below when you need a response. Remember to enter in the priority codes only after punching in the phone number. If you enter 911 before entering the return phone number, it will activate emergency 911.

Enter the pager codes after the number.

1 = high priority   2 = medium priority   3 = low priority

Use 911 as a suffix after the number only if it is a personal emergency.

On Duty/Off Duty Responsibilities:

i85s Equipment –

Non-supervisory staff are required to activate Nextels while on duty. Equipment is to be turned on when they leave their residence and turned off when they return home.

Supervisory staff are required to activate Nextels while on duty. When off duty and contact is needed, then a call to the residence will occur. If not successful, then a call will be made on the Nexel. Therefore, supervisory staff must turn on their Nextels if they are not available by residential phone.

Employees that are on vacation/sick/PTO/compensatory time are not required to carry Nextel equipment.

i550 Equipment –

All i550 users are required to activate Nextels on while on duty. If contact is needed after hours, then a phone call will be made to the residence. It is the option of i550 users to carry two-way equipment after hours.

Employees that are on vacation/sick/PTO/compensatory time are not required to carry Nextel equipment; 155 phone needs to remain at the site.

All employees are responsible for complying with this Operating Procedure. This Operating Procedure is to be strictly adhered to with no deviation. Violation of this Operating Procedure will be cause for disciplinary action, up to and including termination.

_____   _____
Director   Date

Effective Date: 12/01
Revision Date: 04/08/02

Appendix B

Waivers, Releases, Agreements to Participate, Registrations

- Parks and Recreation Volunteer Enrollment Form
- Exigent Circumstances Release Waiver
- Family Waiver
- Volunteer Waiver Statement for Adults 18 and Older
- Waiver and Release and Medical Treatment Release
- Medication Authorization
- Sponsorship Agreement
- Parental Consent Release and Waiver
- Hold Harmless Agreement
- Hold Harmless, Ice Boating/Sailing
- Hold Harmless Release Form (Portable Bleachers)
- Release and Waiver
- Low and High Challenge Course Assumption and Acknowledgment of Risk
- Hold-Harmless Release and Indemnification (Exhibitor/Volunteer)
- Registration Form
- Release of All Claims

Indy Parks and Recreation
Volunteer Enrollment Form
(To process, form must be completed. Please print.)

General Information

Name:_____ Home #:_____ Work #:_____ D.O.B: _____

Other Names (maiden, etc.) _____ Driver's License #: _____

Please check the block if over the age of 64 ☐

Home Address: _____ City: _____

State: _____ Zip Code: _____ County: _____

Previous Address: _____
               Address/City/State/Zip Code

Emergency Contact: _____ Phone #: _____

Volunteer Interests: (check all that apply)

☐ Arts & Crafts   ☐ Aquatics   ☐ Concerts   ☐ Day Camp   ☐ Environmental/Beautification

☐ Facility Maintenance/Improvements   ☐ Greenways   ☐ Major Taylor Velodrome   ☐ Park Facility Volunteer

☐ Park Ranger Cadet   ☐ Park Ranger Fire Team   ☐ Park Ranger Reserve   ☐ School Outreach Program

☐ Senior Programs   ☐ Skate Park   ☐ Special Events   ☐ Sports

☐ Therapeutic & Adaptive Recreation   ☐ Trail Monitor   ☐ Walking Coordinator

Volunteering with Groups: (check all that apply)

☐ Adults   ☐ Preschool   ☐ Persons with disabilities   ☐ Seniors   ☐ Teens   ☐ Youth

Hours and Days of Availability: (check all that apply)

☐ Flexible   ☐ Prefer Weekdays   ☐ Prefer Weekends   ☐ Holidays

☐ Prefer Morning Hours   ☐ Prefer Afternoon Hours   ☐ Prefer Evening Hours

Skill Section: (check all that apply)

Sport Specific Skills:

☐ EMT*
☐ CPR/First Aid*
☐ Timers
☐ Scoreboard Operator
☐ Swimming Instructor
☐ Judge
☐ Coach/Trainer*
☐ Referee*
☐ Other _____

Sport Interest:

☐ Basketball   ☐ Badminton   ☐ Baseball   ☐ Swimming
☐ Ice Hockey   ☐ Volleyball   ☐ Table Tennis   ☐ Softball
☐ Tennis   ☐ Soccer   ☐ Chess   ☐ Bowling
☐ Inline Hockey   ☐ Football   ☐ BMX
☐ Skateboarding   ☐ Power Soccer   ☐ Boxing
☐ Inline Skating (racing)   ☐ Golf
☐ Inline Skating (aggressive)
☐ Senior Olympics

Other Specific Skills:

☐ Computer   ☐ Instructor/Teacher   ☐ American Sign Language Interpreter
☐ Greeter   ☐ Organizing groups/activities   ☐ Language Interpreter _____
☐ Tutoring   ☐ Environmental knowledge
☐ Gardening   ☐ Photography
☐ General Clerical Skills
☐ Other _____

*Please provide evidence of certification or licenses for volunteer file.

Please list two references (not relatives).

Name	Address	Phone #

Name	Address	Phone #

Please read the following information and sign below. (Unsigned and incomplete forms will not be processed)

General Intent

I agree and consent to serve as a volunteer for Indy Parks and further agree that I am not to be regarded as an employee of Indy Parks or entitled to any benefits of employment.

Waiver of Liability

I do knowingly and without reservation hereby agree to release, indemnify and hold harmless the City of Indianapolis and its Department of Parks and Recreation, their members, officers, agents and employees from every liability, claim, loss damage, or expense (including attorney fees) for every injury or damage to property, which injury or person/damage arises out of or is in any way connected with my participation in this event or program.

Image Release

In consideration of _____, my/ my minor child/ ward being allowed to participate in
                              (volunteer name)   (circle one)
any way in the Indianapolis Department of Parks and Recreation sponsored events, programs and activities, the undersigned agrees that such volunteer's likeness may be photographed or videotaped and that such image my only be used to promote or publicize the Department through publication in a Department of Parks and Recreation outlet or other publication.

(If volunteer is under 18, parent or legal guardian must consent to terms and sign below. If volunteer is below 14, parent or guardian must accompany and supervise while child is volunteering.)

*All volunteers must be at least twelve (12) years old to volunteer at Indy Parks and Recreation.

Signature: _____ Date: _____

Parent/Legal Guardian Name:_____ Home Address:_____

City _____ State _____ IN _____ Home #: _____ Work #: _____

Please return form to: Attention to Volunteer Coordinator, Indy Parks and Recreation, 200 E. Washington St., Suite 2301, Indianapolis, IN 46204. Phone # 327-7036.

For Staff Use Only.

Will the individual require a background check conducted based upon their volunteer activity(ies) with Indy Parks and Recreation?

Yes ____   No ____

Date interviewed: _____ By: _____ Park Location:_____

For Volunteer Manager Use Only.

Accepted/Rejected (based upon background check): _____   (revised 1/31/05)

EXIGENT CIRCUMSTANCES RELEASE WAIVER

NAME OF SUMMER LATCHKEY SITE: _____   DATE: _____

I (parent/guardian name), _____ do Hereby
authorize the City of Corpus Christi, Park and Recreation Department to sign out my
child/ren(name),
_____
to (name/s & age/s, _____, who is/are minor/s
because (list reasons):

_____

_____

_____

****NOTE: (Children are not allowed to walk home for any reason)

I will hold the City of Corpus Christi and Park and Recreation staff harmless from all
monetary damages, including punitive damages, imposed by any lawsuit filed related to
any injury my child/ren may receive after being released to the above name minor/s. I
understand that by signing this I give up all rights to sue the City of Corpus Christi and/or
Park and Recreation Staff.

Parent/GuardianName:_____

Address: _____

Phone: _____

OFFICE USE ONLY:

DATE APPROVED/DENIED: _____

COMMENTS:

_____

BLOOMINGTON PARKS AND RECREATION
Family Waiver

I am the parent/legal guardian of the child named below. I recognize that because of the inherent hazards of this activity, my child(ren) and/or I may sustain some injury. In the event that my child and/or I are injured and my spouse or I cannot be contacted, I give my permission to the attending physician to render such treatment as would be normal, and agree to pay the usual charge for such treatment.

I now release the City of Bloomington, its Parks and Recreation Department, and its employees, agents and assigns for any and all claims for personal injury and/or property damage that may arise from, or be in any way connected to, my and my child(ren)'s participation in this activity. I understand that this release applies to both present and future injuries, and that it binds myself, my spouse, my child(ren), and the heirs, executors and administrators of each of these persons. I have read this release and understand all of its terms. I sign it voluntarily and with full knowledge of its significance.

Please list the names of all children for whom the above waiver applies.

_____   _____
Child's Name   Child's Name

_____   _____
Child's Name   Child's Name

_____   _____
Child's Name   Child's Name

_____   _____
Parent / Guardian Signature   Date

_____   _____
Parent / Guardian Signature (if applicable)   Date

_____
Address   City   State   zip

_____   _____
Phone   email

In case of an emergency, please contact:

_____
Name   relationship   phone

BLOOMINGTON PARKS AND RECREATION
VOLUNTEER WAIVER STATEMENT
For Adults 18 and Older

ACTIVITY:_____

I recognize that because of the inherent hazards of this activity, that I may sustain some injury. In the event that I am injured and my next of kin cannot be contacted, I give my permission to the attending physician to render such treatment as would be normal, and agree to pay the usual charge for such treatment.

I now release the City of Bloomington, its Parks and Recreation Department, and its employees, agents and assigns for any and all claims for personal injury and/or property damage that may arise from, or be in any way connected to, my participation in this activity. I understand that this release applies to both present and future injuries, and that it binds my heirs, executors and administrators. I have read this release and understand all of its terms. I sign it voluntarily and with full knowledge of its significance.

_____   _____
Signature   Date

_____
Printed Name

In case of emergency, please contact:_____
                                      Name   Phone   Relationship

CLEVELAND METROPARKS
[Division or name of event can go here]
Waiver and Release

(This form must be completed and returned to the program administrator before any program participation)

Participant's Name _____ Birth Date _____

Parent/Guardian Name (*if applicable*)_____

Address _____

Phone _____ (*Home*) _____(*Business*)

PLEASE READ CAREFULLY
(Provisions in parentheses apply if the waiver is signed for a minor or ward)

As part of the consideration tendered for my (my child/ward) being permitted to participate in [_____*describe activity*_____] on [*dates of service*], I agree (for and on behalf of myself and my child/ward) to, and do hereby, waive any and all claims against, and agree to fully release, hold harmless, and indemnify, the Board of Park Commissioners of the Cleveland Metropolitan Park District, its officers, employees, agents, and volunteers from any and all claims related to any illness, injury, including loss of life, property damage, or loss of any other description which I (or my child/ward) may sustain arising out of, or in any way associated with, my (or my child/ward's) participation in _____.

(If the participant is a minor, the parent(s)/guardian(s) must sign)

_____   _____
Participant   Date   Parent/Guardian   Date

                                                     _____
                                                     Parent/Guardian   Date

MEDICAL TREATMENT INFORMATION MUST BE COMPLETED ON REVERSE SIDE

CLEVELAND METROPARKS
[Division or name of event can go here]
Medical Treatment Release

To Whom It May Concern:

In the event of injury or illness, I authorize (on behalf of myself and my child/ward) Cleveland Metroparks to obtain first aid and/or medical treatment at the nearest and most adequate facility of Cleveland Metropark's choice

Name of Participant: _____

Dates when release is effective: _____
(program dates)

Emergency Contact:

Name_____

Address_____

City, State, Zip_____

Relationship_____   Phone #_____

Medical History:

Special Dietary Needs_____

Do you (or your child/ward) have any allergies, including reactions to insect bites/stings and food? (List)

_____

Are you (or your child/ward) taking any medication? _____

Medication   Reason/Ailment

_____   _____

_____   _____

Any history of medical problems or special circumstances we should be aware of?

_____

_____

Medical Ins. Co. _____Physician/Ph # _____

This release is completed and signed of my own free will with the sole purpose of authorizing medical treatment under emergency circumstances for myself or, in my absence, for the minor child/ward listed.

Signed _____   Phone _____
(by adult participant or guardian of minor child/ward)

Address _____ City/Zip _____

St. Paul Division of Parks and Recreation Medication Authorization for Administration
(Short-term Programs)

The following authorization form must be completed by Parent/Guardian for all short-term programs offered by the St. Paul Division of Parks and Recreation in which medication may need to be administered during the time of activity. This includes field trips, day camp programs, overnight trips, etc.

Name of Participant _____   Birth date _____

Program enrolled in _____   Dates of Program _____

Name of Physician/Licensed Prescriber _____

Clinic Address _____   Clinic Phone _____

Medications include all prescription as well as non-prescription/over-the-counter medications

Medical Condition	Medication	Strength	Dose	Time	Route*	Possible Side Effects

Other Considerations/Directions _____

Start Date _____   Stop Date _____   *Route = Oral, topical, or inhaled

Parent/Guardian Authorization

1. I request that the above medications(s) be given during program hours as ordered by the participant's physician/licensed prescriber.
2. I release St. Paul Parks and Recreation personnel from liability in the event adverse reactions result from the above-named participant taking their medication(s).
3. I give permission for the Program Coordinator to consult with the above named physician/licensed prescriber regarding any questions that arise with regard to the listed medication(s) or medical condition(s) being treated by the medication(s).
4. I give permission for the medication(s) to be given by the staff designated by St. Paul Parks and Recreation for medication and health related concerns during the length of this program.
5. I will notify St. Paul Park and Recreation staff of any change in the medication(s), (ex: dosage change, medication is discontinued, etc.).

_____   _____
Date   Parent/Guardian Signature   Relationship to Participant

Note: Medication is to be supplied in the original/prescription bottle. Non-prescription/Over-the-Counter Medication must be sent in the original container which has an identifiable label.

AA-ADA-EEO Employer

SPONSORSHIP AGREEMENT

The sponsoring business, _____, by its authorized representative, has read the information included in this brochure and agrees to the following sponsorship.

Program / Facility / Event	Level of Sponsorship	Contribution
		TOTAL =

Bloomington Parks and Recreation shall adhere to the sponsoring business' sponsorship agreement. In the event the above named sponsor wishes to terminate sponsorship prior to the event, the sponsor will not be entitled to any refund of the sponsorship fee.

The sponsor agrees to release, hold harmless and indemnify the City of Bloomington, its Park and Recreation Department, and its officers, employees, and agents from any claims or causes of action that may arise under this Agreement as a result of the sponsor's own negligence or other breach of duty. The City of Bloomington Parks and Recreation Department agrees to release, hold harmless, and indemnify the Sponsor and its officers, employees, and agents from any claims or causes of action that may arise under this Agreement as a result of the Parks Department's negligence or other breach of duty; however, such indemnification shall be subject to any and all defenses and immunities provided by Indiana law.

_____   _____
Authorized Representative of Sponsor   Date

_____   _____
Authorized Representative of Bloomington Parks and Recreation   Date

Make checks payable to: Bloomington Parks and Recreation Foundation (if applicable)

SIMPLY COMPLETE THIS FORM AND RETURN IT TO:

Bloomington Parks and Recreation Department   ~ OR ~   Fax your completed form to:
Recreation Services Sponsorship   (812) 349-3705
P.O. Box 848
Bloomington, IN 47402
c/o Kim Ecenbarger

**City of Bloomington
Parks & Recreation**

PARENTAL CONSENT
RELEASE AND WAIVER OF LIABILITY
AND ASSUMPTION OF RISK AGREEMENT

FOR GOOD AND VALUABLE CONSIDERATION, including permission for_____(the "minor") to participate in the following program(s):_____ and related activities, I, the
parent/guardian of the minor, for myself and on behalf of the minor:

1. Consent to the minor's participating in the event or activity;

2. Agree that prior to the minor's participation in the event or activity, the minor and I will inspect the facilities, equipment, and areas where the event or activity is being conducted and. If neither of us believes any of them are unsafe, I will immediately advise the person supervising the event, activity, facility, or area;

3. Acknowledge that the minor and I fully understand that the minor's participation may involve risk of serious injury or death, including economic losses, which may result not only from the minor's own actions, inactions or negligence, but also from the actions, inactions, or negligence of others, the condition of the facilities, equipment, or areas where the event or activity is being conducted, the rules of play or this type of event or activity;

4. Release, waive, discharge, and relinquish the City of Long Beach, and its event and/or activity Permittees and/or Sponsors. And their officers, employees, and agents from any liability, loss, damage, claim, demand, or cause of action against them, attributable to the minor's participation in the event or activity, whether same shall arise by their negligence or otherwise.

5. Assume any and all risks of personal injuries to the minor and authorize the City of Long Beach and/or the event and/or activity Permittees/sponsors to contact or employ a licensed physician to render any medical treatment that may be deemed necessary for the minor or to take and admit the minor to any hospital. I agree to pay all medical and hospital bills relating to such medical treatment or hospitalization, as well as any expenses incurred due to permanent or partial disability, death, or damages to the minor's or my property, caused by or arising from the minor's participation in the event or activity;

6. Covenant not to sue or present any claim for personal injury, property damage, or wrongful death for or on behalf of the minor against the event and/or activity Permittees/Sponsors, the City of Long Beach, or their officers, employees, and agents, attributable to the minor's participation in the event or activity;

7. Agree that photographs, pictures, slides, movies, or videos of the minor may be taken in connection with the minor's participation in the event or activity without compensation from the event and/or activity Permittees/Sponsors or the City of Long Beach and consent to the use of the photographs, pictures, slides, movies, or videos for any legal purpose;

8. FOR MINORS PARTICIPATING IN DAY CAMPS, YOUTH SPORTS, EXTENDED DAY, AND SWIMMING LESSONS: Warrant that the minor is in good health and has no physical condition that would prevent the minor from participation in the event or activity. If the minor does have any restrictions that would prevent the minor from participation in the event or activity, warrant that a "Physical Examination Report" is on file with the City of Long Beach, for review by the City Health Officer;

9. Acknowledge and agree that the City of Long Beach, its officials, employees, and agents shall not be responsible for administering, providing, or assisting in administering medication to or medical assistance of the minor;

10. Acknowledge that the City of Long Beach and event and/or activity Permittees/Sponsors are not joint sponsors, joint venturers, partners, or otherwise jointly engaged in the above-named event or activity.

IMPORTANT: THIS DOCUMENT RELIEVES THE CITY, ITS EVENT AND/OR ACTIVITY PERMITTEES AND/OR SPONSORS, AND OTHERS FROM LIABILITY FOR PERSONAL INJURY, WRONGFUL DEATH, AND PROPERTY DAMAGE CAUSED BY NEGLIGENCE.

BOTH PARENTS MUST SIGN UNLESS ONLY ONE PARENT IS LIVING OR UNLESS ONLY ONE HAS LEGAL CUSTODY. LEGALLY APPOINTED GUARDIANS MUST SIGN AND FURNISH A CERTIFIED COPY OF LETTERS OF GUARDIANSHIP.

I HAVE READ THIS DOCUMENT, UNDERSTAND THAT I WILL GIVE UP SUBSTANTIAL RIGHTS BY SIGNING IT, AND SIGN VOLUNTARILY.

Parent/Guardian Name(s): _____   _____   _____

                    (Print)   (Signature)   (Date)

I HAVE READ THIS DOCUMENT SIGNED BY MY PARENT OR GUARDIAN AND JOIN THE WAIVER, RELEASE, AND ASSUMPTION OF RISK. I AM AWARE OF THE RISKS INVOLVED IN MY PARTICIPATION IN THE EVENT OR ACTIVITY.

Minor's Name _____   _____   _____
          (Print)   (Signature)   (Date)

Hold Harmless Agreement

Between **Chase Manhattan Bank** and the **Monmouth County Park System Board of Recreation Commissioners.**

The **Monmouth County Park System Board of Recreation Commissioners** agrees to release, indemnify and hold harmless **Chase Manhattan Bank** from and against any loss, damage or liability, including attorney's fees and expenses incurred by the latter entities and their respective employees, agents, volunteers, or other representatives, arising out of or in any manner related to the Senior Hiking Program partaking of two hiking outings on Chase Manhattan property adjacent to Middletown Road in Holmdel Township.

The dates of the hiking outings by the Senior Hiking Program are November 3rd and December 13th, 1999.

SIGNED FOR THE MONMOUTH COUNTY PARK SYSTEM BOARD OF RECREATION COMMISIONERS:

SIGNATURE: _____   DATE: _____

WITNESS: _____   DATE: _____

HOLD HARMLESS RELEASE FORM
Ice Boating/Sailing

The applicant hereby certifies that the Manasquan Reservoir was inspected, examined, and found to be clean and without hazard to prospective users and the premises are accepted as suitable for the proposed use.

It is agreed by the applicant that the Monmouth County Board of Chosen Freeholders, Monmouth County Park System, Monmouth County Board of Recreation Commissioners, New Jersey Water Supply Authority and all persons in the employ of said Boards will be held harmless from any liability whatsoever resulting from the use of said Reservoir by or under the auspices of the applicant.

SIGNED:_____

CAPACITY OF:_____

ADDRESS:_____

_____

TELEPHONE NO.:_____

ORGANIZATION:_____

_____

DATE:_____

HOLD HARMLESS RELEASE FORM
(MUST ACCOMPANY APPLICATION)

The TOWNSHIP OF MARLBORO hereby certifies that the portable bleachers have been personally inspected and examined by representatives of the township and found to be without hazard to prospective users. The pick-up, set-up and delivery of the bleachers is the responsibility of Marlboro Township.

The TOWNSHIP OF MARLBORO hereby agrees to hold harmless, defend, and indemnify the Board Of Recreation Commissioners, the County Of Monmouth, their agents, servants, and employees from any and all liability for any loss of life, bodily injury or property damage whatsoever arising from the use of said portable bleachers by TOWNSHIP OF MARLBORO. This covenant shall include the provision of a defense for the above named entities at all stages of the claims or judicial process. The TOWNSHIP shall cause the BOARD OF RECREATION COMMISSIONERS and the COUNTY OF MONMOUTH to be named as additional insureds on any applicable liability insurance policy. Additionally, prior to any event involving the use of said bleachers, the TOWNSHIP OF MARLBORO shall forward to the COUNTY OF MONMOUTH, through its BOARD OF RECREATION COMMISSIONERS, evidence of its status as an additional insured by providing the appropriate policy endorsement from the insurance company writing the liability policy.

TOWNSHIP OF MARLBORO

SIGNED: _____

CAPACITY OF: _____

ADDRESS: _____

_____

TELEPHONE #: _____

DATE: _____

DATES OF USE: _____

City of Long Beach
Release and Waiver of All Liability
and Assumption of Risk Agreement

FOR GOOD AND VALUABLE CONSIDERATION, including permission to participate in
_____ and related activities ("EVENT"), I, for myself, my successors, heirs, assigns, executors, administrators, spouse, and next of kin:

1. Agree that, prior to participating I will inspect the facilities, equipment, and areas to be used, and, if I believe that any of them are unsafe, I will immediately advise the person supervising EVENT, facility, activity, or area;
2. Acknowledge that I fully understand that *my participation may involve risk of serious injury or death*, including economic losses, which may result not only from my own actions, in-actions, or negligence, but also from the actions, in-actions, or negligence of others, the condition of the facilities, equipment, or areas where EVENT or activity is being conducted, the rules of play, or this type of EVENT or activity;
3. *Assume any and all risk* of bodily injuries to myself, including medical or hospital billes, permanent or partial disability, death, and damages to my property, caused by or arising from my participation in EVENT or activity;
4. *Covenant not to sue or present any claim* for personal injury, property damage, or wrongful death against the _____ (PERMITEE/Sponsor), the City of Long Beach, their officers, employees, volunteers, and agents for damages attributable to my participation in EVENT or activity;
5. *Release, waive, discharge, and relinquish* the _____ (PERMITEE/Sponsor), the City of Long Beach, their officers, employees, volunteers, and agents from any liability, loss, damage, claim, demand, or cause of action against them arising from or attributable to my participation in EVENT or activity, whether same shall arise by their negligence or otherwise;
6. Agree that photographs, pictures, slides, movies, or videos of me may be taken in connection with my participation in EVENT or activity without compensation from the City of Long Beach or the _____ (PERMITEE/Sponsor), and consent to the use of these photographs, pictures, slides, movies, or videos for any legal purpose.
7. Warrant that I am in good health and have no physical condition that would prevent me from participating in this event or activity; and
8. Acknowledge that the City of Long Beach or the _____ (PERMITEE/Sponsor) are not joint sponsors, joint venturers, partners, or otherwise jointly engaged in the above-named EVENT or activity.

THIS DOCUMENT RELIEVES THE CITY AND OTHERS FROM LIABILITY FOR BODILY INJURY, WRONGFUL DEATH, AND PROPERTY DAMAGE BY NEGLIGENCE. I HAVE READ THIS DOCUMENT, UNDERSTAND THAT I GIVE UP SUBSTANTIAL RIGHTS AND ASSUME ALL RISKS BY SIGNING IT, AND SIGN VOLUNTARILY.

_____ _____ _____
           PRINTED NAME   SIGNATURE   DATE

Monmouth County Park System
Low and High Challenge Course
Assumption and Acknowledgement of Risk

A challenge course is a series of tasks, obstacles or challenges that participants will travel through, on or around during the course. Many challenges involve physical activity such as crawling, walking, climbing, lifting or other movements. Some of the challenges will be off the ground. On all high challenges, participants are required to wear a harness and helmet and be connected to a safety system.

....

Although the Monmouth County Park System (referred to herein as "MCPS") has taken reasonable steps to provide me with appropriate equipment and/or skilled staff for my program, I acknowledge these programs have risks, including certain risks that cannot be eliminated without destroying the unique character of these programs.

These risks can cause loss or damage to my personal belongings, accidental injury, illness, or in extreme cases, permanent trauma, disability or death.

I understand that the MCPS does not want to frighten me or reduce my enthusiasm for this activity, but thinks it is important for me to know in advance what to expect and to be informed of the program's inherent risks. The following describes some, but not all, of those risks.

- Challenge courses contain environmental risks and hazards including insects and animals; poisonous plants; lightning, snow, wind, rain, and unpredictable forces of nature.

- Possible injuries and illnesses include abrasions, lacerations, strains, sprains, and fractures; insect bites and allergic reactions, and other mild or serious conditions.

I agree to assume responsibility for the inherent risks identified herein and those inherent risks not specifically identified. My participation in this activity is purely voluntary, no one is forcing me to participate, and I elect to participate in spite of and with full knowledge of the inherent risks.

_____   _____
Date   Participant's Signature
                                   (Parent or Guardian if a minor)

_____
Minor's Signature
(ages 17 and under)

CLEVELAND METROPARKS
WAIVER/HOLD HARMLESS/RELEASE AND INDEMNIFICATION

PLEASE READ CAREFULLY

In consideration for my being permitted to participate as an exhibitor/volunteer at _____, on or about_____, I agree to and do hereby waive any and all claims against, and agree to fully release, hold harmless, defend and indemnify, the Board of Park Commissioners of the Cleveland Metropolitan Park District (Cleveland Metroparks), their officers, agents, representatives, and employees from any and all claims, losses or expenses, including reasonable attorney's fees, resulting from any injury, including loss of life, property damage, or losses of any other description which I may sustain and/or which may be sustained by any other person or property arising out of or in any was associated with my activity as a exhibitor/volunteer.

Prior to commencing any exhibitor/volunteer activity at Cleveland Metroparks, I will forward a certificate of insurance or other acceptable documentation from an insurance carrier or agent evidencing my procurement of liability insurance acceptable to Cleveland Metroparks and including Cleveland Metroparks as an additional insured. Without limiting the generality of the foregoing, such coverage shall be primary to any insurance carried by Cleveland Metroparks, shall provide limits satisfactory to Cleveland Metroparks, and shall reflect not less than ten (10) days prior written notice to Cleveland Metroparks of cancellation, non-renewal or material change of said insurance.

VOLUNTEER/EXHIBITOR'S NAME (Please Print)

_____

VOLUNTEER/EXHIBITOR'S SIGNATURE

_____

ADDRESS   _____

_____

DATE   _____

City of
Corpus
Christi

Registration Form

Corpus Christi Park & Recreation Department
(MUST FILL OUT COMPLETE FORM or child may be disqualified from the program.)

Site:_____ Date of Birth:_____ Age:_____ Sex:_____ Grade:_____

Name:_____ Email:_____

Address:_____ City/Zip:_____

Parent/Guardian (P/G):_____ Phone (H):_____ (W):_____

Alternate Emergency Contact:_____ Phone (H):_____ (W):_____

Medical Information:_____

Special Needs:_____

Child's Physician:_____ Address:_____ Phone:_____

For Latchkey Summer Camps Only:

Important: Please *LIST ANY AND ALL PERSONS AND THEIR PHONE NUMBERS* that will be allowed to sign your child out of the Summer Program (children will only be released to those listed). All authorized persons must present a picture I.D. The City reserves the right to refuse the child to any person listed and/or remove any person listed from the list if circumstances so warrant.

Name:_____ Ph.:_____   Name:_____ Ph.:_____

Name:_____ Ph.:_____   Name:_____ Ph.:_____

Name:_____ Ph.:_____   Name:_____ Ph.:_____

Immunization Records

Child's Name:_____

Attends (during school year):_____ Address:_____ Phone:_____

His/her immunization record is on file at the school and tuberculosis test results are current. I have also been provided with a Parents Guide to Day Care.

Parent/Guardian's Signature:_____ Date:_____

Acknowledgement

☐ Yes, I received the Latchkey information brochure, understand and will abide by all policies and guidelines. _____ Initials

While supplies last.
Youth Size:
☐Medium ☐Large

T-Shirt Size
☐Small ☐Medium ☐Large

While supplies last.
Adult Size:
☐XLarge ☐XXLarge

Medical Release/Waiver

I (Parent/Guardian),_____, do hereby authorize the City of Corpus Christi Park and Recreation Department to provide emergency medical treatment to my child,_____, in the event that I am unreachable and in the event of an emergency need for such treatment. I further authorize the treatment to be provided by the licensed medical practitioner or facility determined by the staff to be the best able to serve my child's needs, and further; I understand that I am totally responsible for any expense associated with such treatment. The safety of my child is always the City's number one concern. I understand that every effort will be made to contact me or the person who has been designated by me as soon as practical after such an occurrence. I hereby agree not to sue the City of Corpus Christi if my child is injured in any manner while participating in said program. I will hold the City of Corpus Christi and staff harmless from all monetary damages, including punitive damages, imposed by any lawsuit filed related to any injury my child may receive while participating in said program. I understand that by signing this I give up all rights to sue the City of Corpus Christi.

Address:_____ Phone:_____

Parent/Guardian's Signature:_____ Date:_____

Field Trips

My child,

_____,
has permission to participate in the following: (check the appropriate boxes)
A. Off campus water activities
☐ Yes ☐ No
B. Off campus field trips
☐ Yes ☐ No

Photographic Release

I hereby do _____, do not _____, consent and authorize the Corpus Christi Park and Recreation Department to reproduce photographs or video of my child for advertising and publicity purposes of every description.

_____ _____
P/G's Signature   Date

Request for Special Accommodations

My signature is proof that I have received a copy of the Request for Special Accommodations Packet.

_____ _____
P/G's Signature   Date

Survey to Better Serve You

How did you hear about our programs? Check all that apply. Thank you.
☐Flyer ☐Newspaper ☐TV ☐Radio ☐Word of Mouth/Friend ☐Called Park & Recreation

FOR OFFICE USE ONLY: Latchkey Camp Hours 7:30a.m.–6:00p.m., Monday-Friday / Date of Admission:

FOR OFFICE USE ONLY: Name:

Group:

RELEASE OF ALL CLAIMS

For the sole and only consideration of the sum of _____
_____, I (we), the undersigned _____
_____ do hereby release, settle, cancel, discharge and acknowledge to be fully satisfied any and all claims, demands, derivative claims, rights and causes of action of every kind, nature or description whatsoever, both known and unknown, suspected or unsuspected, which may now or hereafter have or assert against the BOARD OF PARK COMMISSIONERS OF THE CLEVELAND METROPOLITAN PARK DISTRICT, (referred to as "Cleveland Metroparks" or against any other person, firm, association, political subdivision, corporation or entity arising out of, or by reason of, or in any manner connected with an accident occurring on or about _____ at or near
_____.

This Release and the receipt of any consideration hereunder are not intended to be, and are not deemed to be, any evidence of any admission of liability on the part of Cleveland Metroparks, or anyone else, but constitute a compromise and settlement of disputed claims.

I/We acknowledge that I/we have entered into this Release and settled all of my/our claims voluntarily, based upon my/our own judgment and not in reliance upon any representation or promise made by anyone acting for or on behalf of Cleveland Metroparks other than those contained in this Release.

IN WITNESS WHEREOF, I/we have hereunto signed my/our name(s) to the foregoing Release this ____ day of _____, 200_, and am/are aware that this Release includes a release of all known and unknown claims.

Signed in the presence of:

_____   X_____
Name

Address: _____   X_____

_____

STATE OF _____
                                    SS.
COUNTY OF _____

On the ____ day of _____, 200_, before me personally appeared _____
_____ to me known to be the person(s) named herein and who executed the foregoing Release, and __ he __ acknowledged to me that __ he __ voluntarily executed the same.

_____
Notary Public

My commission expires: _____

Appendix C

Use Permits, Rentals

- Facility Use Application
- Special Events or Filming Application
- Use of City Streets or Public Property
- Permit to Berth/Moor a Vessel
- Ice Arena Rental Confirmation
- Aquatic Center Rental Confirmation
- Pool Rental Request
- Facility Rental Policy
- Rental Reservation Form
- Community Center Facility During Hours Use Application Permit
- Community Center Facility After Hours Use Application Permit
- Rental Building Rules
- Special Use Permit Application
- Rental Letter of Agreement
- Collections of Damages Procedures

City of Foster City Parks and Recreation Department
Estero Municipal Improvement District

FACILITY USE APPLICATION

Recreation Center
650 Shell Blvd.
Foster City, Ca. 94404
(650) 286 – 3380
Fax # (650) 345-1408

Library Community Center
1000 E. Hillsdale Blvd.
Foster City, Ca. 94404
(650) 286 – 2500
Fax # (650) 638-1936

NAME OF INDIVIDUAL/ORGANIZATION _____

DATE(S) OF EVENT: _____, _____, _____ THROUGH _____
     (Day of the Week)   (Month & Date)   (Year)   (Month, Date, and Year)

If you are requesting multiple dates, please attach a listing of all requested dates.

START TIME: _____ END TIME: _____ (Include activity, set-up, prep. & clean-up time)

PURPOSE OF ORGANIZATION: ___ Foster City Resident ___ Non-Resident ___ Foster City Non-Profit ___ Government Agency

___ Foster City Business ___ Non-Resident Business ___ Non-Resident, Non-Profit ___ City Use

PURPOSE OF EVENT: ___ Private Party ___ Meeting ___ Public Event ___ Fundraising ___ Employee Training

ATTENDANCE: _____ WILL ALCOHOL BE SERVED? ___ Y ___ N TO BE SOLD? ___ Y ___ N PERMIT #_____

SET-UP REQUESTED (please circle one): U-Shape   Square   Classroom   Theatre Style   Other (see set-up chart)

EQUIPMENT REQUESTED BY APPLICANT: _____

FACILITY REQUESTED:

RECREATION CENTER

___ Spray Room   ___ Mallard Room
___ Mist Room   ___ Gull Room
___ Bluebird Room   ___ Crane Room
___ Bluebird Kitchen   ___ Spirit Room
___ Lagoon Room w/veranda & kitchen

LIBRARY COMMUNITY CENTER

___ Wind Room
___ Port Room
___ Starboard Room

OTHER FACILITY _____

In submitting this Application, I certify that I have read and understand the guidelines for facility use and will abide by any special conditions set forth. I certify that the intended use, as detailed above, is in compliance with said rules and regulations, application instructions and any specific use regulations and subject to advance payment of all rental fees, security deposit, certification of insurance requirements (if required) and approval by the Director of Parks and Recreation, or designated supervisor. I understand and agree that the City retains the right to cancel this permit at any time. APPLICANT ACKNOWLEDGES THAT THEY ARE RENTING A PUBLIC FACILITY AND AS SUCH, THE CITY CANNOT GUARANTEE ACTIVITIES SURROUNDING THE BUILDING THAT MAY IMPACT PARKING, SOUND OR VIEW.

Applicant hereby agrees to hold the Estero Municipal Improvement District, The Parks and Recreation Department, The City of Foster City, the individual members thereof and all district and city agents and employees free and harmless from any loss, damage, liability, cost or expense that may arise during or be caused in any way by such use or occupancy of said facility. The applicant agrees to furnish such liability and/or other insurance for the protection of the public and the district as the district may require. Applicant also agrees to leave the facility in the same condition as found before use.

(Print Name)	(Title/Office Held)	(Signature)	(Date)
(Street Address)	(City & Zip Code)	(Home Phone)	(Work Phone)

OFFICE USE ONLY

ITEM	HOURS	RATE	TOTAL
_____	_____	@ $_____	= $_____
_____	_____	@ $_____	= $_____
_____	_____	@ $_____	= $_____

Security Deposit $_____ Date_____ Received By____
Insurance $_____
Rental Fee $_____
Equipment Fee $_____
Total Charges $_____

Received By _____ Approved By_____ Date:_____

Date Deposit Sent to Finance_____

Balance of Fees $_____ Due Date:_____ Received By_____

Posted By_____ Date_____ Set Up Submitted_____

CITY OF LONG BEACH

DEPARTMENT OF PARKS, RECREATION & MARINE - SPECIAL EVENTS & FILMING

One World Trade Center. Suite 300 • Long Beach, CA 90831 • (562) 570-5333 FAX (562) 570-5335

To the Special Event or Film Applicant:

This informational letter and the attached General Liability endorsement form are intended to assist you in obtaining the insurance coverage required for your event/activity and permit. **Please forward this letter and the City's General Liability Endorsement from to your insurance broker-agent.**

For the duration of your permit, you must maintain, from an insurance company(ies) either admitted to write insurance in the State of California or rated A:VIII by A.M. Best Company (or equivalent), the following insurance coverages, unless the City's Risk Manager determines that other coverages or higher limits are required for your specific event or activity:

1. **Commercial general liability** (equivalent to ISO CG 00 01 11 85 or CG 00 01 11 88) in an amount not less than One Million Dollars ($1,000,000) per occurrence. If food is sold, products liability coverage in an amount not less than One Million Dollars ($1,000,000) must be included. If alcoholic beverages are sold or served, liquor liability coverage in an amount not less than One Million Dollars ($1,000,000) must be included. If participants, film extras, and/or spectators are involved, the certificate of insurance must specify that the commercial general liability covers participants, film extras, and/or spectators as applicable. The City's **General Liability Endorsement** form provides coverage for the City, its officials, employees, volunteers, and agents as additional insureds under your commercial general liability policy.

2. **Workers' compensation** as required by the California Labor Code, if the permit holder uses its own employees in conducting the planned event/activity/film shoot.

3. **Automobile Liability** (equivalent to ISO form CA 00 01 06 92) in an amount not less than One Million Dollars ($1,000,000) combined single limit covering Symbol 1(Any Auto), if automobiles are used in the move-in, setup, break-down, or operation of the event/activity/film shoot. If you are using only nonowned or hired autos, a nonowned auto endorsement to your general liability policy is acceptable.

4. **Aircraft Liability** in an amount not less than One Million Dollars ($1,000,000) per occurrence, if helicopters or other aircraft are used in the conduct of or in connection with the event/activity/film shoot.

5. **Watercraft Liability** in an amount not less than One Million Dollars ($1,000,000) per occurrence, if watercraft are used in the conduct of or in connection with the event/activity/film shoot:

You must provide to this office at least twenty (20) working days prior to your event/activity/film shoot:

- Certificate of Insurance issued by your insurance broker-agent evidencing the insurance coverages applicable to your event/activity/film shoot, with the cancellation provision on the certificate amended to read as follows: "Should any of the above described policies be canceled before the expiration dates thereof, the issuing company will mail thirty (30) days prior written notice to the certificate holder. In the case of cancellation for nonpayment of premium, the issuing company will mail ten (10) days prior written notice to the certificate holder."

- *City's General Liability Endorsement* completed by your insurance company or insurance agent;

- Any written statements by you and/or your insurance broker-agent explaining the reasons why any of the above coverages are limited or why any of the applicable requirements have not been satisfied.

All certificates and endorsements must be original, signed documents submitted to **JoAnn Burns, Director of Special Events, City of Long Beach, One World Trade Center, Suite 300, Long Beach, CA 90831.**

If you or your insurance broker-agent have any questions regarding these insurance requirements, please do not hesitate to contact this office. For your convenience, we have a facsimile machine within this department. **The facsimile access telephone number is (562) 570-5335.**

CITY OF LONG BEACH

DEPARTMENT OF PARKS, RECREATION & MARINE – SPECIAL EVENTS & FILMING

One World Trade Center, Suite 300 • Long Beach, CA 90831 • (562) 570-5333 FAX (562) 570-5335

USE OF CITY STREETS OR PUBLIC PROPERTY

PERMIT APPLICANTS:

Please include with your completed application:

- $25 permit application fee payable to the City of Long Beach

- Petition signed by all residents/business owners within the proposed blocked area. (Please refer to the enclosed SAMPLE PETITION format.)

- Rough map of the blocked area showing barricade placement, alleys, cul-de-sacs or any other public areas specific to your proposed closure. Festivals and elaborate activities must provide a detailed layout and parking plan, as applicable.

- For neighborhood block parties and basic use, please provide a brief description of your event, including any unusual activity (example: children's "moon" bounce, live bands, pony rides, street dancing). More elaborate events will require a detailed proposal and site plan at the time to be submitted with the permit application.

Street barricades are available through Public Service/Street Maintenance at no charge if picked-up, properly placed and returned undamaged by the applicant. Specific barricade information will be included with your approved permit.

If you have any questions regarding the application for street use or any of the listed requirements, please Contact this office at (562) 570-5333. Please allow 5-10 days for permit processing.

CITY OF LONG BEACH
SPECIAL EVENTS & FILMING BUREAU

CITY OF LONG BEACH

DEPARTMENT OF PARKS, RECREATION & MARINE - SPECIAL EVENTS & FILMING

One World Trade Center, Suite 300   •   Long Beach, CA 90831   •   (562) 570-5333   FAX (562) 570-5335

APPLICATION FOR PERMIT
USE OF CITY STREETS OR PUBLIC PROPERTY

_____   _____
(your name)   (street address)

_____, am applying
(city)   (zip code)   (telephone)

for permission, on behalf of_____
                              (name of organization)

to conduct_____
                              (type of event to be held)

at_____   _____
              (proposed event location)   (anticipated attendance)

on_____ from _____
              (date)   (time: set-up to tear-down)

It is my understanding that in applying for permission to use City streets, the permit, when approved will be subject to the following conditions. I further understand that application must be **received** by the Park, Recreation & Marine's Office of Special Events 10 work days in advance of block parties, 20 work days in advance for other uses of streets.

1.   The street will be posted, coned or barricaded by the organization in a manner which clearly warns **all** vehicular traffic of the closure, while still allowing ready access to emergency vehicles. The city Traffic Engineer and the Chief of Police must approve the manner in which this is done.

2.   The premises (streets, parkways, alleyways and sidewalks) must be cleared of any debris, signs, cones or barricades immediately after the event has been held.

3.   Our organization will hold the City harmless from any liability caused by the conduct of the event. The City will not be liable for any mishaps or injuries associated with the event. Full responsibility for activities at the event will be assumed by the organization. It is my understanding that the City may require evidence of insurance if appropriate.

4.   Our organization will be responsible for all costs incurred by City departments for use of City personnel and/or equipment. The costs will be submitted to the Office of Special Events for payment as appropriate.

5.   Our organization will not allow fireworks of any sort during the conduct of our event.

6.　The City will not allow live bands or amplified speakers to be used during the conduct of our event unless specifically authorized by the Office of Special Events.　Approval will be based on permission by the Noise Specialist/ Environmental Health Officer of the Health Department, in conjunction with the Noise Control Ordinance.

7.　NO ALCOHOLIC BEVERAGES WILL BE CONSUMED IN PUBLIC OR ON PUBLIC RIGHTS-OF-WAY.

_____
(APPLICANT SIGNATURE)

Please return this form to: JO ANN BURNS, MANAGER OF SPECIAL EVENTS, City of Long Beach, One World Trade Center, Suite 300, Long Beach, CA 90831
Telephone: (562) 570-5333　•　Fax　(562) 570-5335

FOR APPLICATION EVALUATION ONLY

APPLICATION RECEIVED BY: _____ DATE: _____ FEES PAID: $_____

Request for Recommendation for Approval/Denial of Permit:	Recommend Approval	*Recommend Denial
_____	_____	_____
_____	_____	_____
_____	_____	_____
_____	_____	_____

*Reason for denial or special requirements by involved City departments must be returned to this office in writing.

Special requirements for conduct of event which must be provided by sponsor/applicant prior to date the event is held:

_____
_____
_____
_____

PERMISSION APPROVED　　　　　　　　PERMISSION DENIED

_____　　　　　　　　　　　_____

_____　　_____
JO ANN BURNS, MANAGER OF SPECIAL EVENTS　　DATE

SAMPLE PETITION

Dear Applicant,

Your petition must be circulated among all residents/businesses within the proposed street closure. If you encounter vacant property please identify the appropriate property as VACANT.

APPLICANTS MUST HAVE UNANIMOUS CONSENT FROM ENTIRE BLOCK.

PETITION FOR STREET CLOSURE

We the undersigned are aware of and agree to the closure of _____

Street (include block number and name of street) on _____ (date),

from _____ to _____ (duration). We understand _____

_____ (Name of group) will be using the area for the

purpose of _____ (type of activity).

STREET ADDRESS	ADULT SIGNATURE
_____	_____
_____	_____
_____	_____
_____	_____
_____	_____
_____	_____
_____	_____

CITY OF LONG BEACH
Parks, Recreation & Marine
205 Marina Drive, Long Beach, CA 90803
(562) 570-3215
Fax: (562) 570-3247

Permit #:
Slip/Mooring #:
Slip Length: ft.

Permit for Slip

PERMITTEE INFORMATION		VESSEL INFORMATION			
Name:		Boat Name:		Boat #:	
Residence:		Deck Length:		Overall Length:	
City/State:	Zip:	Beam:	Draft:	Type:	Sail
Phone:		Bowsprit:		Davits:	
Business Name:		Swim Step:		Other:	
Address:		Builder:		Material:	Fiberglass
City/State:	Zip:	Name of Engine:		H.P.:	
Bus. Phone:	Ext.:	# of Motors:		Seaworthy Inspection:	
Boat Phone:	Pager:	Fuel Type:	Gas	Bureau LOA:	
Cellular Phone:					

Remarks: Liveaboard: NO 0 person(s)

Partners: NO 0 partner(s)
Partnership Statements issued, to be notarized and returned by:

The undersigned, having applied for a permit to berth/moor the above-described vessel at the Long Beach marinas, acknowledges that the granting of permission to use and occupy slip/mooring number   at Alamitos Bay Marina does not and shall not be construed as the grant, conveyance or transfer of an interest in real property; that neither this permit nor any interest herein may be transferred except in accordance with the provisions of the Long Beach Municipal Code and the Long Beach Marina Rules and Regulations, and that the undersigned's use and occupancy of slip/mooring number   may be terminated by the Manager of the Marine Bureau after notice to the undersigned of the undersigned's failure to observe and comply with the provisions of the Long Beach Municipal Code and the Rules and Regulations, policies and procedures ("applicable regulations") governing and controlling the administration and operation of the Long Beach marinas. The undersigned further acknowledges that he/she has read and understands the applicable regulations and that the applicable regulations are subject to change. The undersigned in his/her use and occupancy of the assigned slip/mooring, agrees to comply with and be bound by the applicable regulations now in force and as hereafter changed. The undersigned certifies that the information set forth above is true and correct and that the situs of his/her vessel is and shall be the City of Long Beach.

SPECIAL CONDITIONS:
Waiver: The Permittee waives all claims for damage to persons and/or property sustained by Permittee on or about Permittee's vessel or within the Downtown Shoreline Marina or the Rainbow Harbor Marina resulting from oil operations conducted on Island Grissom, and neither the City of Long Beach nor any of its officers, employees, or contractors shall be liable for any such claim for damage to persons and/or property. All property belonging to Permittee located at said marinas shall be there at the risk of Permittee, and the City shall not be liable for damage thereto nor theft or misappropriation.

NOTICE OF CANCELLATION MUST BE RECEIVED *IN WRITING BY THE FIFTH* (5TH) DAY OF A CALENDAR MONTH IN ORDER TO BE EFFECTIVE ON THE LAST DAY OF THAT MONTH.

DATE: SIGNATURE: _____

MARINE BUREAU USE ONLY

Effective Date:
Original Date:
Permit Type: ORIGINAL
Monthly Permit Fee:
Security Deposit:
Liveaboard Fees: per month
Key Deposit:
Total Fees: Invoice #:
Rate Change: NO

Received By: Pam Cunningham, Marina Agent III

Approved: _____
              (Marina Supervisor/Marina Agent III)

Approved: _____
              (Marine Bureau Superintendent/Manager)

COLUMBUS PARKS AND RECREATION DEPARTMENT
HAMILTON CENTER ICE ARENA
25th Street and Lincoln Park Drive, P. O. Box 858
Columbus, IN 47202-0858
Phone: (812) 376-2686

HAMILTON CENTER ICE ARENA RENTAL CONFIRMATION

Name of Organization _____

Contact Person _____ Phone (___)_____

Billing Address _____ People expected #___

Date of Rental _____ Time from _____ to _____ Area _____

Date of Rental _____ Time from _____ to _____ Area _____

Date of Rental _____ Time from _____ to _____ Area _____

Date of Rental _____ Time from _____ to _____ Area _____

Check if desired: *Concession Stand* ___Yes ___No   *Broomball Equipment Rental $15./Hr.* ___Yes ___No

LARGE RINK	**SMALL RINK**	***OVERNIGHT**	**PATIO**
$130./Hr. *In-County*	$55./Hr. *In-County*	**LOCK-INS** *(Fri. only)*	**ONLY**
$150./Hr. *Out-of-County*	$65./Hr. *Out-Of-County*	$600. (11 pm - 5 am)	$25./Hr.

FEE FOR LARGE RINK and SMALL RINK RENTAL does not include rental skates. Skate rental fee is **$1.50 per person**. The small rink is available for small skating groups only *(20 or less)* and for broomball games.

FEE FOR OVERNIGH LOCK-INS includes large rink rental, rental skates, a building supervisor, on-ice guards and a skate rental attendant. Available Friday pm / Saturday am **only** from December through March. Does **not** include small rink rental or broomball equipment.

RENTAL AGREEMENT
1. It is mutually understood that approval of the above request in no way places the Parks and Recreation Department in a position of liability for any injuries of participants, that may result from the approved usage.
2. The individual acting on behalf of an organization requesting the usage agrees to be in attendance throughout the stated hours and dates of rental and to be responsible to the Parks and Recreation officials for the proper conduct of those in attendance and for the proper care of the Hamilton Center facility.
3. It is understood that any damage to facilities or equipment which might occur through other than normal wear and tear will be the responsibility of the user to restore to original condition. *Overnight Lock-Ins require a $100. security deposit which will be returned if the facility is left in a clean and orderly manner.
4. No alcoholic beverages are permitted. Smoking is not permitted inside Hamilton Center.
5. Balance of rink rental is due on the date of rental unless other billing arrangements are made prior to rental.
6. Cancellation must be made at least 30 days in advance. Failure to give at least 30 days notice of cancellation will result in a forfeit of rental deposit fee. Failure to cancel 10 days before event will require full payment for scheduled ice time, weather being an exception.

Date Reservation Taken _____ *(Taken in Person ___ Taken over Phone ___)* Taken by_____

_____   _____
Management Signature   **Customer's Signature**

A **$25. Deposit** is required for each rental date, balance is due day of rental.

Checks made payable to **Columbus Parks and Recreation Dept.**
P. O. Box 858
Columbus, IN 47202-0858

Deposit $_____	Balance $_____	Skate Rental $_____	*Chg. Name_____
Ck__ Ca__ Chg__ *	Ck__ Ca__ Chg__ *	Ck__ Ca__ Chg__ *	Acct.#_____
Date _____	Date _____	Date _____	Date _____

COLUMBUS PARKS AND RECREATION DEPARTMENT
22ND AND SYCAMORE STREETS, P.O. BOX 858
COLUMBUS, IN 47202-0858
(812) 376-2680

Copy Distribution:
White - Aquatics Mgr.
Canary - Customer
Pink - Pool Mgr.
Gold - Donner Center

DONNER AQUATIC CENTER RENTAL CONFIRMATION

Name of Individual/Organization_____

Contact Person_____ Phone ( )_____

Billing Address_____ Zip Code_____

Event_____Purpose of Event_____

Date(s)_____Time(s)_____Total Time_____

Attendance Expected_____Admission Charge_____Proceeds Used for_____

Concession Stand____Yes ____No   Caterer____Yes ____No

GENERAL RENTAL AGREEMENT

1. It is mutually understood that approval of the above request in no way places the Parks and Recreation department in a position of liability for any injuries of participants which may result from the approved usage.

2. The individual or person acting in behalf of an organization requesting the usage agrees to be in attendance throughout the stated hours and dates of usage, and to be responsible to Parks and Recreation officials for the proper conduct at Donner Pool.

3. It is understood that any damage to facilities or equipment which might occur as a result of this usage will be the responsibility of the user to restore to original condition to owner's satisfaction.

4. It is understood that all food and beverages for events at Donner Aquatic Center are to be purchased from the concession stand or the Parks and Recreation Department caterer.

5. A deposit is required at the time of reservation. No time will be reserved without a deposit, and no deposit will be refunded unless cancellation is made by the Friday two weeks prior to the event. The deposit will be refunded if the pool is unavailable due to weather, mechanical failure, or other similar event.

6. No rental confirmation will be issued until full payment of a rental fee is made. Full payment for services and rent is due no later than 12 Noon, two days prior to the scheduled usage; and is payable to the Columbus Parks and Recreation Department, 22nd and Sycamore Streets, P.O. Box 858, Columbus, IN 47202-0858.

RENTAL FEES: DONNER AQUATIC CENTER

$75.00 per hour: Intended for a small party (100 people or less). The party will be allowed to use all areas of the pool: Diving Well, Slide, Leisure Pool and Main Pool.

$90.00 per hour: The rental group (not to exceed 200) will be allowed to use all areas of the pool: Diving Well, Slide, Leisure Pool and Main Pool.

$100.00 per hour: The rental group (200 plus) will be allowed to use all areas of the pool: Diving Well, Slide, Leisure Pool and Main Pool.

OFFICE USE ONLY

Date Reservation Taken_____ Taken in person_____ By Phone_____ Taken By_____

_____   _____
Manager's Signature   Renter's Signature

Deposit Fee $_____ Date Paid_____ Check____Cash____ Received by_____

Usage Fee $_____ Date Paid_____ Check____Cash____ Received by_____

IOWA CITY RECREATION DIVISION
POOL RENTAL REQUEST

Date of Application _____

Contact Person _____

Address _____

Phone: Day _____ Evening_____

Date Requested _____

Time Requested _____

Estimated Attendance _____

Estimated number of participants with limited swimming skills _____

Please describe your group (i.e., scout troop, birthday party) _____

_____

Please note any assistance you need with scout badges or other pertinent information

_____

_____

FACILITY REQUESTED

☐ **Recreation Center Pool**
   ($50/2 hr. minimum use
   plus staff cost*)

☐ **Recreation Center Pool**
   ("Rent the Rec" special - Sundays
   1-3 p.m. fee $35/2 hours -
   no staff cost)

☐ **Mercer Park Aquatic Center**
   ($75/hour plus staff cost*)

☐ **City Park Pool**
   ($50/hour plus staff cost*)

*Staff cost will vary depending on
the size and type of group.
Minimum cost for a 2 hour use
would be $22.00.

All rents are due and payable seven (7) working days prior to use. The Recreation Division Office is open between 8 a.m. and 7 p.m., Monday through Thursday, and Friday between 8 a.m. and 5 p.m. Return with remittance to Iowa City Recreation Division, 220 S. Gilbert Street, Iowa City, Iowa.

- -

FOR OFFICE USE ONLY

Request Approved _____ Confirmation Sent_____

Pool Rules Sent _____ Fee Received _____

Receipt No. _____ Date Fee Received _____

JOLIET PARK DISTRICT
FACILITY RENTAL POLICY

It is the intent of the Joliet Park District to provide use of its recreational facilities on a fair and equitable basis while demonstrating the best possible use of the facility.

Reservations will be scheduled and fees assessed in accordance with the policies and procedures listed below.

1. All scheduling will be assigned with the following priority:

   A. Joliet Park District sponsored event
   B. Event co-sponsored by the Joliet Park District
   C. Affiliated clubs/groups
   D. Not-for-profit groups or individuals
   E. For-Profit Businesses and For Profit Activity

   as determined by the following definitions:

   * **JOLIET PARK DISTRICT SPONSORED EVENT** - activities and special events organized, planned and sponsored by the Joliet Park District. Proceeds of the event are paid to the Joliet Park District.

   * **EVENT CO-SPONSORED by JOLIET PARK DISTRICT** - activities or special events planned in accordance with Park District standards and open for participation by any resident of the District. Organization and planning of the activity or event done jointly with the District staff.

   * **AFFILIATED CLUBS/GROUPS** - activities of the club must be in accordance with Park District standards and open for participation by any resident of the District with use of facilities as is provided to other residents of the District. Organization and planning determined by the group or club with administrative guidance of the District and an annual financial statement must be provided to the District. Either the proceeds of the event or rental fees are paid to the Joliet Park District.

   * **NOT-FOR-PROFIT GROUPS OR INDIVIDUALS** - private use groups and organizations neither sponsored nor affiliated with the District and operate independently of the District guidelines, but meet the criteria as a not-for-profit organization or private exclusive use. Non-profit groups must possess a 501C3 designation by the IRS. Examples include but are not limited to athletic teams, school and church groups, and private party rentals. Rental fees are paid to the Joliet Park District

   * **FOR PROFIT GROUPS** - individuals or groups independent of the District demonstrating a desire for exclusive use of a room, court, gymnasium, etc. for profit use. For Profit Businesses are included in this group *even if the activity being offered is free to the public.* Examples include but are not limited to trade shows, seminars and private business rentals. Rental fees are paid to the Joliet Park District.

page 2
Joliet Park District
Facility Rental Policy

2. ***The rental of a Joliet Park District facility by groups/individuals is for occasional use and not intended to create a permanent or regular site for said users. Therefore, the Joliet Park District reserves the right to limit the frequency of all rentals.***

3. The Park District assumes no responsibility for any accident or loss of property.

4. No permit will be issued to individuals or groups for a <u>regularly</u> scheduled rental when charging fees or admission for the purpose of monetary gain.

5. Requests for meetings or activities involving minors (18 years and under) must be made by an adult representing the group who will be present throughout the course of the activity scheduled in the facility.

6. All individuals or groups using the facility are responsible for clean-up and will leave the area in a clean and orderly fashion. Additional clean-up and damage charges will be billed to the individual signing the request if the facility is not returned to its original condition.

7. Alcoholic beverages are not allowed in any of the Recreational facilities. Special arrangements can be made, however, to serve alcohol at functions held at the Horticultural Center. ***At no time may alcohol be brought in by the renter.*** Any rental is subject to cancellation without refund if alcohol is found on premises during a non-alcohol rental.

    The Joliet Park District reserves the right to require additional security and damage deposits depending on the size of the group, the nature of the event and when groups using the Nature Center and Horticultural Center will be serving alcohol.

8. SMOKING IS PROHIBITED IN ALL JOLIET PARK DISTRICT FACILITIES.

9. Only the Joliet Park District and its authorized vendors are permitted to sell concessions. Permission to sell concessions or vended items during a rental can only be granted by the Board of Commissioners. Special request to do so must be put in writing and submitted with the rental request.

10. In appropriate cases, as determined by the District, the user may be required to supply the District with a certificate of insurance naming the Joliet Park District additionally insured in the sum of $1 million.

Page 3
Joliet Park District
Facility Rental Policy

11.   In appropriate cases, as determined by the District, the user may be required to provide any of the following:

-    Provisions for adequate security.
-    A formal outline of the event including attendance estimate, parking requirements and seating requirements.
-    All permits or licenses as determined by the City of Joliet.

12.   All decorating plans, use of signs/banners, etc. must be approved by the District prior to the activity being held. Absolutely no confetti or glitter.

13.   Use of loud speakers or P.A. systems must be authorized by the District on a per use basis.

14.   For profit groups can be required to pay a percentage of ticket sales, registration fees or vendor fees as is appropriate and as determined by the District.

15.   *The District reserves the right to refuse or cancel use by any organization whose use is not conducive to the facility, as determined by the District.*

Revised 1/1/02

JOLIET PARK DISTRICT
FACILITY RENTAL APPLICATION

FACILITY LOCATION _____   ROOM
REQUESTED _____

REQUESTED
DATE(S) _____

DAY(S) _____ TIMES _____ to _____

DESCRIPTION OF ACTIVITY _____

ESTIMATED ATTENDANCE _____   AGES ATTENDING _____

SET UP/DECORATING REQUEST _____

ADDITIONAL REQUESTS (if any) _____

The availability of tables and chairs is limited at each facility. Please contact the manager to determine the number of tables and chairs available for your rental.

TYPE OF ORGANIZATION   AFFILIATED _____   NON-PROFIT/PRIVATE _____   PROFIT _____

NAME OF ORGANIZATION/CLUB/INDIVIDUAL _____

PERSON IN CHARGE _____   TITLE _____

ADDRESS _____   PHONE (Home) _____
(Work) _____
CITY _____   (Cell) _____

STATE _____   ZIP CODE _____

A non-refundable deposit fee of _____ must accompany this application. Balance of the rental fee is due three days before the event. The individual signing for the permit is responsible for the event/activity and will be billed for additional charges and damages in accordance with the fee structure.

TOTAL RENTAL _____   DEPOSIT _____   BALANCE DUE _____

The Joliet Park District assumes no responsibility for injury or loss of personal property. It is recommended that participants make provisions for this coverage with their own insurance.

I HAVE READ THE POLICIES AND PROCEDURES/FEES AND CHARGES OF THE JOLIET PARK DISTRICT AND AGREE TO ABIDE BY THEM AND UNDERTAKE RESPONSIBILITY FOR THE ABOVE ACTIVITY.

_____   _____
DATED   SIGNATURE OF REPRESENTATIVE

_____   _____
DATED   JOLIET PARK DISTRICT SIGNATURE

City of Bloomington Parks & Recreation
P.O. Box 848
Bloomington, IN 47401
(812) 349-3700

Banneker Community Center	Bloomington Adult Community Center	Jukebox Community Building
930 West 7th Street	349 South Walnut Street	349 South Washington
(812) 349-3735	(812) 349-3720	(812) 349-3731

RENTAL RESERVATION FORM

Name: _____ Date of Reservation:_____

Address: _____ City/State:_____

Home Phone:_____ Work Phone: _____

Facility Requested:

☐   Banneker Community Center   ☐   Bloomington Adult Community Center

☐   Jukebox Community Bldg.

Time: From_____ to _____

Nature of Activity/Event:_____Anticipated Attendance _____Will there be an admission fee charged? ☐Yes ☐ No   If yes, state amount_____Will the event be catered? ☐ Yes ☐ No If yes, by whom? _____*We have read, fully understand, and agree to abide by the rules, regulations, and restrictions governing the use of said facility and agree to be responsible for any damage to park property due to such occupancy and for the strict observance of the rules and regulations of the Bloomington Parks and Recreation Board of Park Commissioners relative to the use of the facility. The renter assumes all risk of loss, damage or injury to persons or property. Bloomington Parks and Recreation Department is thus released from all claims for such loss, damage or injury sustained while the renter uses the facilities.*

_____   _____
_Signature   Printed Name

_____
_Address   City   State   Zip   Date

For Office Use Only:	Damage Deposit
	Date Paid _____
	Receipt #_____

Rental Fee:_____

Deposit: _____ Date Paid: _____ Receipt #_____

Balance Due:_____ Date Paid: _____ Receipt #_____

Confirmed by:_____ Date: _____
                Facility Coordinator

THE MARYLAND-NATIONAL CAPITAL PARK AND PLANNING COMMISSION,
DEPARTMENT OF PARKS AND RECREATION, PRINCE GEORGE'S COUNTY

COMMUNITY CENTER FACILITY DURING HOURS USE
APPLICATION PERMIT

Name of Organization/User Group: _____

Name of Contact Individual: _____

Address: _____
       Street   City   State   Zip

Telephone: Home: (_____)_____   Work: (_____)_____

Are you a resident of: ❏ Prince George's County   ❏ Montgomery County

. . . .

Center Requested: _____

Room(s) Requested: _____ Equipment Requested: _____

Date(s) Requested: _____ Hours Requested: From _____ to _____
                                                   (am/pm)   (am/pm)
                                              includes set-up and clean up

GROUP: Please Check	PURPOSE: Please Check	ACTIVITY: Please Check
❏ Recreation Council/Affiliate ❏ School ❏ Service Organization ❏ Community Group/Civic & Social ❏ Governmental ❏ Religious ❏ Other _____	❏ Private/for Profit ❏ Not for Profit ❏ Non-Profit ❏ Other _____ Are you charging a fee? ❏ No ❏ Yes	❏ Recreational ❏ Community Service ❏ Cultural ❏ Social ❏ Workshop/seminar ❏ Educational ❏ Scholarship ❏ Other _____

PURPOSE OF ACTIVITY: _____

_____

Expected number of Participants _____

FUNDRAISERS AND PRIVATE SOCIAL FUNCTIONS ARE PROHIBITED.
THE CONSUMPTION OF ALCOHOLIC BEVERAGES IS PROHIBITED.

In submitting this application, I hereby confirm that I am familiar with the Rules & Regulations governing during hours use of community centers.

_____   _____
       Date   Signature of Contact Individual

FOR OFFICE USE ONLY
. . . . **DO NOT WRITE BELOW THIS LINE** . . . .

                                                        ❏ Affiliate/Recreation Council

                                                        ❏ Non-Profit & Not For Profit

Quarter: ❏ Jan-Mar ❏ Apr-Jun ❏ Jul-Sep ❏ Oct-Dec   ❏ Private/For Profit

     Application to be submitted 30 days prior to event   Fees: $ _____
                                                    Attach copy of check or money order
Recommendation for Approval: payable to: M-NCPPC

_____ ❏ Yes   ❏ No   Comments: _____
 Facility Director   Date
_____ ❏ Yes   ❏ No   Comments: _____
 Regional Manager   Date

Final Approval: _____   ❏ Yes ❏ No
               Program Superintendent   Date

           Applicant-White Copy   Facility-Yellow Copy   Area Office-Pink Copy   Rev 5/98

During Hours Use of M-NCPPC Community Centers

Dear User Group:

Effective July 1, 1998, the Commission is instituting a fee structure which governs the use of Community Centers by organizations during the Center's normal hours of operation.

Private Schools
Meeting/Class Room — $35.00/hr
Gymnasium — $85.00/hr

Non Profit & Not for Profit
Meeting/ Class Room — $10.00/hr
Gymnasium — $30.00/hr

Affiliates & Recreation Councils
No charge

All of this is subject to space availability and programmatic functions of the facility, under the following terms:

- Application - Submitted through the Facility Director 30 days prior to the event. The Director does not have final approval, but will make recommendation to the Division Office via the Regional Manager.
- Form of Agreement - By written application for Quarterly periods. January-March/April-June/July-September/October-December.
- Scheduling - Commission activities will not be postponed or canceled to make facilities available to other groups. All group use shall be subject to Commission scheduled activities and we reserve the right with proper notification to cancel activities in case of a conflict or emergency.
- Assurance - An individual agency, organization or group will furnish the Commission, upon request, the following information:
    - A copy of the articles of incorporation, charter, by-laws, State and Federal Tax Exempt certificates and/or other documents indicating the legal status purposes of the organization,
    - A statement of use for the property or facilities requested, and
    - Record of insurance coverage and other information as requested.
- Permittees are required to abide by all applicable Federal, State, and/or County public laws in accordance with the M-NCPPC Park Rules & Regulations.
- Inspection - An inspection shall be made prior to and immediately after use to determine if damage to the facility has resulted. Groups and/or individuals will be requested to compensate the Commission for any damages incurred during their use.
- Possession and consumption of alcoholic beverages will not be permitted.
- Kitchen use is limited to storage only - no food preparation allowed.
- Time Limitation - Open during scheduled operating hours only.
- Permits for use of Community Centers are issued to adults only and are on a first-come first-service basis.
- Cancellation of Activity - Notification at least 72 hours in advance; within 72 hours of the activity, there will be a forfeiture fee equal to one hour's rental fee, if applicable.
- User groups will be responsible for setting up and taking down tables and chairs. User groups will also be responsible for clean up after use.
- Solicitation and/or fundraisers of any kind is strictly prohibited.
- Rental Fees - The Facility Director shall compute applicable charges. The total number of hours shall include time requested for setup and clean up.
- Payment - All fees are to be paid by check or money order, made payable to M-NCPPC and shall accompany the application for use.

FUNDRAISERS AND PRIVATE SOCIAL FUNCTIONS ARE PROHIBITED
CONSUMPTION OF ALCOHOLIC BEVERAGES IS PROHIBITED

**THE MARYLAND-NATIONAL CAPITAL PARK
AND PLANNING COMMISSION
DEPARTMENT OF PARKS AND RECREATION
PRINCE GEORGE'S COUNTY**

COMMUNITY CENTER FACILITY AFTER-HOURS USE
APPLICATION AND PERMIT

Date of Application _____

Name of Organization _____

Name of Contact Individual _____

Address _____
         Street   City   State   Zip

Telephone: Home _____ Work _____

Are you a Bi-County Resident Yes ☐   No ☐   ☐ Prince George's County   OR   ☐ Montgomery County

Center Requested _____

Room(s) Requested _____

Date Requested _____ Hrs. Requested: From _____ To _____

Activity _____

Is a fee being charged? Yes ☐   No ☐   If yes, for what purpose?

_____

Expected number of participants_____

Is permission being requested for possession and consumption of alcoholic beverages? Yes ☐   No ☐
(if yes, note Items 10 and 11 of Concise Information.)

In submitting this application, I hereby confirm that I am familiar with the Rules and Regulations Governing After-Hours Use of Community Centers, as well as The Maryland-National Capital Park and Planning Commission's Rules and Regulations for the Use of Park Property and Facilities.

In addition, applicant/permittee agrees to indemnify and hold harmless the Commission from and against all actions, liability, claims, suits, damages, cost or expenses of any kind which may be brought or made against the Commission or which the Commission must pay and incur by reason of or in any manner resulting from injury, loss or damage to persons or property resulting from his/her negligent performance of or failure to perform any of his/her obligations under the terms of this application/permit.

_____   _____
        Date   Signature of Contact Individual

– **Do Not Write Below This Line** –

Recommendation of   Damage Deposit $ _____
Facility Director

                                  Estimated Rental Fee $ _____

Approval _____ Disapproval _____   Service Fee $ _____

Comments _____

Date _____ Signature _____

Recommendation of Division Chief's Office

Approval _____ Disapproval _____

Comments _____

Date _____ Signature _____

Action by Director's Office

Approval _____ Disapproval _____

Comments _____

Date _____ Signature _____
                                   Associate Director

Date _____ Signature _____
                                   Director of Parks and Recreation

CONCISE INFORMATION

1. While the Commission desires to make available the facilities under its control for proper public functions, it is felt that the applicant should be familiar with the Rules and Regulations and share with the Commission a responsibility for correct and proper usage.

2. **Application**–Submitted through the Facility Director one (1) month prior to the event.

3. **Approval**–Usage is contingent upon final approval of the Department Director or his designee.

4. **Scheduling**–Commission activities will not be postponed or cancelled to make facilities available to other groups.

5. **Assurance**–Said individual, agency, organization or group will furnish the Commission, upon request, the following information:

   A. A copy of the articles of incorporation, charter, bylaws, or other documents indicating the legal status and stated purposes of the organization; and

   B. A Statement of the use to be made of the property of facilities requested; and

   C. Statement of Insurance Coverage; and

   D. Financial statement for approved fund raising events; and

   E. Other information as required.

6. **Inspection**–An inspection shall be made prior to and immediately after use to determine if damage to the facility has resulted.

7. **Rental Fees**–The Facility Director shall compute applicable charges. The total number of hours shall include time required for setup and cleanup.

	Bi-County	Non Bi-County
Gymnasium	$60.00 per hour	$72.00 per hour
Meeting Room	$40.00 per hour per room	$48.00 per hour per room
Kitchen	$25.00/permit	$25.00/permit
Entire Building	$85.00 per hour	$100.00 per hour
		(Bi-County Resident - Those who reside in Prince George's or Montgomery County)

7a. **Service Fee**–$13/hr. for those groups who are not charged a rental fee as outlined in the Rules and Regulations Governing After-Hours Use of Community Centers and it is not a fund-raising activity. (see # 11)

8. **Payment**–All fees are to be paid by check or money order, made payable to The Maryland-National Capital Park and Planning Commission, and shall accompany the application for use.

9. **Damage Deposit**–An amount not to exceed $200.00 may be required upon confirmation of reservation at the discretion of the Facility Director.

10. **Overtime**–Any user group remaining after the permitted time will be assessed any amount equal to one-half hour rental for any portion of an additional one-half hour use.

11. **Fund Raisers**–Fund raisers shall be limited to recognized organizations, whose primary purpose is to promote park and recreational activities which are generally available to the public; and with all proceeds being returned to the local community or community center to be used for park and recreation programs, including equipment. The Director of Parks and Recreation shall make final determinations regarding eligibility. Fund raisers will be assessed a fee of $25/hr. for this use. **Non Bi-County residents are not eligible.**

12. **Alcoholic Beverages**–Prohibited except to those groups authorized for fund raisers. (See Rules and Regulations Governing After-Hours Use of Community Centers.)

13. **Form of Agreement**–By written application.

14. **Security**–At the discretion of the Facility Director, one or more State of Maryand deputized, uniformed police officers may be required. Payment of police services IS NOT INCLUDED as part of the Community Center rental fee and is the specific responsibility of the user. Confirmation that a law enforcement officer has been obtained must be given to the Facility Director at least 72 hours in advance or the event may be cancelled.

15. **Time Limitation**–No function will continue after 12:00 Midnight. Exceptions may be granted up to 2:00 a.m. by the Director of Parks and Recreation or his designee.

16. Permittees are required to abide by all Federal, State and/or County public laws and ordinances arising from use of facilities.

17. Permits for use of Community Centers are issued to adults only and are on a first-come, first-serve basis.

18. **Collection of Fees**–Prohibited except for approved Fund Raisers.

CHAMPAIGN COUNTY FOREST PRESERVE
RENTAL BUILDING RULES

1. Furnishings are not to be removed from buildings or shelters for any reason.

2. Smoking is not permitted in any Forest Preserve District buildings or on the Golf Course Clubhouse deck.

3. Staples, nails, tacks, brads, or other holding devices cannot be used as they will damage buildings and kill trees. Decorations, signs or other such materials may be secured to the building with tape or string. Signs that are placed in the park to give directions need to be secured on wooden stakes rather than taped to garbage cans and sign posts.

4. Balloons and other small bits of refuse can be eaten by wildlife and may kill them. Rice and confetti are not allowed because of the danger to wildlife, but bird seed may be thrown outside buildings. Water balloons and the intentional release of helium balloons are not allowed. If balloons are used for decoration please make sure that no materials, including uninflated balloons, are left on the ground where wildlife can find them.

5. It is common that the District has other renters coming in on the day following your rental, leaving us with little time to properly prepare the facility for their arrival. All decorations, signs, sidewalk chalk, or other materials, either inside a building or outside, must be removed before your departure. Tables and chairs, and picnic tables must be properly cleaned and returned to the area from which they were taken. CCFPD is unable to furnish cleaning materials other than running water, so please bring them with you.

6. Buildings and shelters are rented "as is". Any additional items must be furnished by the renter. Buildings are furnished with rectangular tables and metal folding chairs adequate for the building capacity. Renters may provide their own tables and chairs if others are preferred, but the number MUST NOT exceed the building's Life Safety Code (maximum capacity). Some electrical equipment such as soda machines, extra refrigerators, large cookers, etc. may exceed the electrical capacity available. Please call Headquarters to make sure the facility will accommodate your needs. The District cannot be responsible for personal property. Your property must be removed at the time of departure.

7. For the protection and preservation of District property, as well as the safety and general welfare of the public, dunk tanks, horseshoes, carnival-type rides, inflatable playhouses, pony rides, etc. are prohibited on District property. *THE ERECTION OF TENTS ON DISTRICT PROPERTY IS PROHIBITED.*

8. Carbon dioxide and helium tanks can be dangerous. They must be placed on their sides or secured to a fixed object to prevent falling.

9. Depending upon the activity, some groups may be required to provide additional covered dumpsters and portable toilets. Groups may be required to pay for additional electricity (presently available only at Lake of the Woods Pavilion and Elk's Lake Pavilion). Please contact Headquarters for requirements.

10. All garbage must be placed inside a container. These containers are provided around and inside of the rental buildings and shelters. If you anticipate a large amount of trash, please notify Headquarters at 586-3360.

11. Departure time specified on reservation sheet is to be actual departure time. LATE departure will result in FORFEITURE of damage deposits.

12. No fires are to be built anywhere, for any purpose, except in provided fireplaces, or in appropriate receptacles. Grills are not to be placed under the overhangs of the buildings, under the roof of a shelter or used on any deck or balcony at any of the preserves.

13. The person or persons renting the building or shelter are responsible for any damaged or missing equipment. If keys are lost, the renter will be assessed appropriate fees to change locks and issue new keys to employees so that the building or shelter will remain secure.

OVER

14. Key Returns:
    Lake of the Woods County Park Building will be unlocked & locked by park personnel as per the rental agreement time.
    Middle Fork River Forest Preserve rental keys are to be deposited in the green locked box (has $1 printed on it), which is located by the firewood area by the campground host trailer, at the time of departure.
    Salt Fork River Forest Preserve rental keys are to be left in the building at the time of departure.

15. All activities must be conducted in a manner that respects the rights of other users or neighbors of the preserves. All pets are to be under direct physical control of a responsible person at all times. Amplifiers must be adjusted at a level that does not intrude on persons 75 feet from the building. NO AMPLIFIED MUSIC IS ALLOWED OUTSIDE THE BUILDING.

16. A damage deposit is required for any rental. The following will be cause for the forfeiture of all or a portion of the damage deposit:
    1. A late departure from the rental facility (rental times are identified on the reservation sheet);
    2. Erection of a tent, dunk tank, inflatable playhouse, or other prohibited items on District property (Please check in advance with CCFPD staff to determine whether or not your intended activity is approved by the CCFPD. Failure to obtain approval may be cause for forfeiture of your damage deposit).
    3. Damage to the facility incurred during the rental; or
    4. Violation of the Life Safety Code by exceeding the facility's maximum occupancy or otherwise.

    The Champaign County Forest Preserve District in no way intends to limit its ability to seek damages in excess of the amount of the damage deposit in the event appropriate, but specifically identifies these factors as the basis for its ability to forfeit an entire security deposit. Should some type of damage accidentally occur to a building or shelter being rented, please notify the Park Ranger or Headquarters as soon as possible.

17. Outside catering (i.e. pig roasts, etc.) must provide for containment and disposal of grease, carcasses and other food production wastes. Such wastes must not be deposited in preserve trash containers, driveways, walks, grass areas, sinks, stools, or drains. Outside caterers must not place grills or cookers on sidewalks, on decks or balconies, under the overhangs of the buildings or under the roof of a shelter. Please contact Headquarters about the placement of cooking devices.

18. Alcoholic beverages may be consumed if confined to the area and served with a meal. All groups consuming alcoholic beverages must provide the District with proof of "Dram Shop Act" or "Host Liquor Liability" insurance in the amount of $1 million. The District must be named as an "additional insured" on the policy. The proof of insurance must be an original and signed by the agent (no copies or faxes accepted). No person under the age of 21 shall be allowed to consume alcohol on District property. The Forest Preserve District may, at its discretion, require renters to pay for the hiring of police officers to enforce Illinois statutes pertinent to alcohol dispensing and consumption.

19. In order that our visitors are free to enjoy our preserves, soliciting contributions or offering items for sale is prohibited.

20. Facility users are also subject to District Ordinance #77-1, General Forest Preserve District Rules and Regulations. (Copies are available upon request.)

21. The rental fee, excluding the $50/$100 reservation fee, will be refunded if notice of cancellation is given at least 30 days prior to the scheduled date of use. Please note that the $50/$100 reservation fee may be refunded in the event that the District is able to rent the facility following your cancellation.

22. Inclement Weather: We have no control over the weather. If your event is scheduled outdoors, you should make contingency plans in case of inclement weather. We do not have alternates available. The District cannot refund your rental fee nor reschedule your event to another date. As customary the damage deposit will be returned.

23. Park hours are from 7 a.m. until sunset or as each of the park's personnel designates.

Revised 10/01

SPECIAL USE PERMIT APPLICATION

This application is made to the Champaign County Forest Preserve District to obtain a Special Use Permit to conduct the activity by and on behalf of the Sponsor Group, all as described herein:

1. Name, address and phone number of Sponsor Group: _____

    _____

2. Name, address and phone number of individual(s) responsible for organizing and on-site supervision of the activity: _____

    _____

3. Type and detailed description of the activity for which Permit is sought. If the activity has been previously conducted by this   or any other organization, state when and where this was conducted: _____

    _____

4. The exact date and times during which the activity will be conducted. Include the expected arrival and departure times of

    both the representatives of the Sponsor Group and, if different, of the participants and spectators: _____

    _____

5. Identify the park, and portion thereof, and any building where the activity is sought to be conducted: _____

    _____

6. Anticipated number of: (A) Sponsor Group Workers: _____   (B) Participants: _____   (C) Spectators: _____

7. Number of vehicles expected: _____   Number and type of vehicles to be used by Sponsor Group on-site with this
    activity: _____

8. Please list the anticipated special needs of the participants and spectators for this activity (i.e. first aid, standby ambulance, crowd control, portable restroom facilities, access to electricity, relocation of trash barrels, etc.), and how the Sponsor Group intends to meet these needs: _____

    _____

9. The undersigned representative of the Sponsor Group acknowledges that the Champaign County Forest Preserve District requires, as a condition of issuance of this Special Use Permit, that **the Sponsor Group submit an original Certificate of Insurance which names the Champaign County Forest Preserve District as the additional insured, for liability in the amount of $1,000,000.**

10. By executing this Agreement, the Sponsor Group agrees to provide all of the personnel and services in connection with this activity as detailed above, to abide by all District rules and regulations, and further agrees to indemnify, defend and hold harmless the Champaign County Forest Preserve District, its officers, agents and employees from any and all claims, including reasonable attorney's fees, resulting from injuries, including death, damages and loss sustained by anyone arising out of, connected with, or in any way associated with the activity for which this application is being made.

11. The Sponsor Group requests the Champaign County Forest Preserve District to consider this application and to contact its representative should any additional information or clarification be required.

_____
Representative of Sponsor Group

_____   _____
Title   Date

St. Louis County Department of Parks and Recreation

LETTER OF AGREEMENT

IT IS UNDERSTOOD AND AGREED THAT WITH THE RENTAL OF [name of facility] ON [month/day/year] FOR THE {name of event], **ST. LOUIS COUNTY DEPARTMENT OF PARKS AND RECREATION (COUNTY)** SHALL:

1. Reserve the right to limit or prohibit access to designated areas.

2. Always have the right to eject any person(s) from the site for any reason that in the opinion of the **COUNTY** deems sufficient.

3. Not hold the [name of organization] **(USER)** responsible, nor shall **USER** hold **COUNTY** responsible, for the nonperformance of this agreement caused by any casualty.

4. Provide set-up of all equipment provided by the **COUNTY.**

5. Reserve the right to collect a per-car parking fee from those in attendance.

IT IS UNDERSTOOD AND AGREED THAT WITH THE RENTAL OF [name of facility] ON [month/day/year] FOR THE [name of event], **USER** SHALL:

1. Guarantee and assume full and exclusive responsibility for all damages to property, fixtures, and equipment belonging to or used by the **USER** at or in the vicinity of the facility if caused by its respective members, opponents, guests, or spectators during the periods covered by the agreement.

2. Shall maintain and keep in force general liability insurance during the duration of the rental period [month/day/year]. **ST. LOUIS COUNTY shall be named as additional insured, in the amount of not less than $300,000 per person / $2,000,000 per occurrence combined single limit for bodily injury and property damage. Coverage shall include products completed operations, if food, beverages or products are sold.** The Certificate of Insurance should include a waiver of subrogation in favor of St. Louis County. **USER** will cause to be issued, and filed with the Department of Parks and Recreation, a certificate of such insurance containing the aforementioned coverage as well as the issuing insurance company giving the **COUNTY** thirty (30) days written notice in advance of any changes or cancellation or non-renewal.

3. Indemnify and hold the **COUNTY**, its officers, agents and employees harmless for all complaints or suits made or brought for injury to persons or property caused by **USER** or **USER**'s members, guests, opponents, or spectators and for any and all losses, claims, damage, costs and expenses arising out of or resulting from any act or omission of **USER** or **USER**'s members, guests, opponents or spectators during the period of this agreement.

4. Comply with all reasonable rules and regulations established and posted by **COUNTY** from time-to-time at the site for which **COUNTY** furnishes a copy to the **USER.**

5.   Provide the **COUNTY** with a base payment of [amount] for the use of reserved facilities and labor associated with the use of [name of facility]during the [event].

6.   Provide appropriate emergency medical facilities during the event.

7.   Provide the appropriate amount of uniformed, licensed security (i.e. County Police or County Park Rangers) during the event (not less than two persons). Contact [name of chief park ranger] [phone number] to arrange for security. Security personnel shall be paid prior to the event. Provide a minimum of four (4) volunteers to assist with parking. Appropriate traffic control outside of the [facility] must be coordinated with County Police.

8.   Obtain the appropriate amount of portable restrooms required to service the estimated crowd (one per every 250 people, of which one of every ten must be handicapped accessible). A copy of the service contract must be provided to the **COUNTY** no later than [month/day/year].

9.   Obtain and have on file with the **COUNTY** the Special Events Permit required by the St. Louis County Department of Health.

10.   Obtain any and all permits required by **COUNTY**, and other local agencies or state agencies.

11.   Police all refuse and return the facility to its original condition. Provide a low- sided dumpster for trash removal. A copy of the service contract must be provided to the **COUNTY** no later than [month/day/year].

12.   Comply with the Americans with Disabilities Act of 1990.

13.   This agreement is not subject to change; a new agreement will be required.

By the signature of duly authorized agent of the St. Louis County Department of Parks and Recreation and [name of organization] for the above commitments agreed upon:

_____   _____
St. Louis County   [name of organization]
Department of Parks and Recreation

_____   _____
Date   Date

COLLECTIONS OF DAMAGES PROCEDURES

Purpose

To explain the procedure on processing a damage report after Facility Rental/Usage.

Procedure

Facility Procedure.

1. After the usage of a facility if there is excessive cleaning required or physical damage then the Facility Manager must assess the situation fill out a Security & Incident report form. See form in S:/Risk Management/Accident and Incident Reporting.

2. The report should include the amount required to render the facility back to the condition before the rental.

3. If there is physical damage or evidence of criminal activity then the Risk Manager must be contacted for further direction.

4. All reports and support documentation, quotes, estimates, pictures, etc to be sent to Risk Manager.

5. Risk Manager after reviewing the documentation for accuracy and completeness will send a copy of documentation to Parks Finance for billing to customer. The Risk Manager will also e-mail the Facility Manager of the final costs due Parks.

6. The manager of the facility needs to notify the customer of damages.

7. An invoice, which includes the estimate for the damages, amount of the security deposit and the balance that is due is issued to the customer by Parks Finance.

8. The customer has 30 days to pay in full.

9. After 30 days has past without payment, a copy of all documentation will be sent from Parks Finance to the City Collection Department. Park Finance will add "Alert Tex" to customer account.

10. Finance will notify Facility Manager and Risk Manager if paid or if sent to collections.

Note: Damage deposits that were made with cash or check can only be refunded by an official city issued check.
Damage deposits made with credit cards will be refunded by credit card credit only.

Effective 03/15/05   **Updated 10/23/07**

Appendix D

Accident and Medical Treatment-Related Forms

- Statement of Admissions
- Ambulance Transportation of Minors
- Accident Reporting Procedures
- Personal Injury Report Form
- Authorization for Medical Treatment and Release from Liability Form
- Authorization to Consent to Medical Treatment for Minor Child
- Consent for Giving of Medications
- Employee Guide for Work-Related Injuries and Illnesses

STATEMENTS OF ADMISSION
(CHAMPAIGN COUNTY FOREST PRESERVE DISTRICT)

When an accident occurs, no mater how insignificant it may seem to be, it is of the utmost importance never to admit to guilt or negligence of any kind until there is a formal investigation of the matter by your supervisors and the causes of the incident have been determined. You are required to contact your immediate supervisor and not to render speculation on the causes of the incident. Any and all questions relating to an accident involving District property and/or personnel must be directed to a department head or other designated manager.

_____   _____
Name   Date

Risk Management Policies - 6030

Date: August 6, 1998   **Accreditation Standard #:**

POLICY RE: **Ambulance Transportation of Minors**

In any case that a minor is involved in an accident that requires an ambulance transport, a staff member should accompany the minor to the hospital or care center if the other children in the program will still be adequately supervised by a staff member. If the minor's parent(s) are on site, the responsibility is transferred to the parent, and the staff member should remain with the other children. The employee should immediately notify their direct supervisor if a participant is injured and requires ambulance transport.

Risk Management Policies - 6020

Date: August 6, 1998   Accreditation Standard #: 3.4.2.3; 9.6

POLICY RE: Accident Reporting Procedures

Employee Accidents
- ALL on-the-job injuries need to be immediately reported to a supervisor. Report of Accident Forms (Employee, Supervisor, Witness [when applicable]) need to be completed for every injury or accident. After supervisor review, copies of the reports shall be routed to the Director of Operations and Development and the Risk Management Division within 24 hours.

- Forms are available in the main office in the Showers Building.

- Under the City of Bloomington's Worker's Compensation policy, employees injured on the job should go to PromptCare or 1st Health Care for treatment. For after hours injuries or emergencies, the employee should seek treatment at the Bloomington Hospital Emergency Room. Any follow up treatment should be done at PromptCare of 1st Health Care.

- Any medical treatment performed by the employee's personal physician will not be covered by worker's compensation.

- When the injured employee returns to work, they must have a doctor's release stating what work they are physically capable of performing and restrictions to their work activity.

    - The Supervisor's Report of an Accident form is completed in the case of damage to city property.

    - The Accident Report is for bodily injury.

    - Witnesses' Report of Accident form is for any witnesses to the accident who are not members of the Bloomington Parks and Recreation Department.

Vehicle Accidents
- All employees driving department vehicles must hold a current operator's license.

- In the event of an accident, call the police. Regardless of the location or severity of the accident, do not move any vehicles prior to the Police arriving at the scene. Secure names, addresses, and phone numbers of persons involved in the other vehicle(s), and any witnesses.

- Do not admit responsibility or sign any statements of any kind. Refer questions about fault and payment to City Risk Management. Immediately report the accident to the supervisor, and fill out Report of Accident forms.

Bloomington
Parks and Recreation

Risk Management Policies - 6020

Date: August 6, 1998   Accreditation Standard #: 3.4.2.3; 9.6

Visitor Participant Accidents
- Inform supervisor immediately.

- Inform Division Director/Safety Director.

- Inform Risk Management.

- Fill out the Accident Report form completely, and route to the Director of Operations and Development within 24 hours. Take the time to gather information - names, addresses, witnesses, etc. that would be helpful in follow-up accident investigations. Fill out the form completely and legibly.

Employee Safety
- Make sure first aid kits are kept fully stocked. Call ZEE Medical if kits need to be restocked.

- If any site is in need of employee safety equipment (safety glasses, traffic vests, ear protection) contact the Director of Operations and Development.

- Employees who are engaged in the following activities may not wear shorts:
    - Using mowing equipment - tractors, push mowers, trimmers.
    - Working in construction zones.
    - Working around or driving heavy equipment.
    - Working around or with pesticides or herbicides.

- All employees are required to wear shirts. Tank tops and safety vests do not count as shirts.

A copy of Risk Management guidelines and sample accident forms follows.

PERSONAL INJURY REPORT FORM

Send top two (2) copies to Risk Management Office

To be used for reporting injuries to patrons or others not employed by the Commission

Date
of Accident: ___ / ___ / ___

Time
of Accident: ____ : ____

AM ☐
PM ☐

Facility/
Location: _____

INJURED PERSON INFORMATION:

Name: _____ Age: _____ Phone: _____

Street: _____ Apt #: _____

City: _____ St: _____ Zip: _____

Parent/Guardian (if under 18): _____

THE INJURY

Nature and Extent of Injury: (Check body part injured)

☐ Face   ☐ Ear (including hearing)   ☐ Eye   ☐ Nose   ☐ Mouth   ☐ Scalp   ☐ Skull

☐ Neck   ☐ Arm (above wrist)   ☐ Wrist   ☐ Hand   ☐ Fingers   ☐ Abdomen   ☐ Back

☐ Chest   ☐ Hips   ☐ Shoulders   ☐ Trunk (other)   ☐ Genitals   ☐ Other

☐ Legs (above ankle)   ☐ Ankle   ☐ Foot   ☐ Toes   _____

Treatment Provided: _____

HOW WAS INJURY CAUSED?   (brief statement)

Struck or injured by: _____

Strain or injured by: _____

Cut, puncture, scrape
injury by: _____

Fall or slip injury by: _____

Striking against or
stepping on: _____

Caught in or between: _____

Burn (heat or cold)
exposure: _____

Foreign body in eye: _____

By animal or insect: _____

Heat stroke/heat
exhaustion: _____

Heart Attack: _____

Stroke: _____

Other: _____

WITNESS:

Name: _____ Phone: _____

Address: _____

ADDITIONAL DESCRIPTION OF ACCIDENT: (include where accident occured) (attach additional sheets if necessary)

_____

_____

Property Damage: ☐ No   ☐ Yes   (If yes, attach property damage form)

Reported by: _____ Title: _____

Date of Report: _____ Supervisor: _____

Risk Management Use Only

Date Received _____   Date Reviewed _____   Initials _____

CITY OF BLOOMINGTON
DEPARTMENT OF PARKS AND RECREATION

Date/Year: **(ex. Jan 15, 2002-Dec 31, 2002)**

Authorization for Medical Treatment
and Release from Liability

Program participant's name: _____

Program participant's date of birth: _____ _____ _____

The undersigned is the adult Program Participant, or is the parent or legal guardian of the Program Participant.

The undersigned hereby states that he/she understands the activities that will take place in this program, and that the Program Participant is physically and mentally able to participate in this program.

As with any activity, there is a risk of injury to the Program Participant. In the event that the Program Participant sustains an injury in the course of this program, and the City of Bloomington Parks and Recreation Department is unable to contact the appropriate person(s) to obtain consent for treatment, the undersigned hereby authorizes the City of Bloomington Parks and Recreation Department and/or its employees or volunteers to take all reasonable steps to obtain appropriate medical treatment for the Program Participant, and authorizes any and all medical providers to render such treatment. The Program Participant and/or his/her parent or legal guardian shall be responsible for the cost of such treatment.

The Program Participant is taking part in this program at his/her own risk. The undersigned agrees to release, hold harmless, and indemnify the City of Bloomington and its employees and volunteers from any claim that may be brought by or on behalf of the Program Participant as a result of his/her participation in this program. This includes, but is not limited to, claims for personal injuries and property damage.

I have read this release and understand all of its terms. I agree with its terms and sign it voluntarily.

Complete either (A) or (B)

(A)

_____   _____
Signature of Adult Participant (18 and over)   Today's Date

<u>Witness Statement</u>: I hereby certify that I have reviewed this release with the Program Participant. I am satisfied that the Program Participant understands this release and has agreed to its terms.

_____   _____
Witness signature   Date

_____   _____
Printed name   Relationship to Program Participant

(B)

_____   _____
Signature of parent/legal guardian   Date

_____
Printed name

department of PARKS & REC

Columbus Parks and Recreation
22nd and Sycamore Streets
P.O. Box 858
Columbus, IN 47202
(812) 376-2680

We're excited to have your child with us for the free summer playground program this year! Please fill out, sign, and return the following forms for our records. Thank you!

Authorization to Consent to Medical Treatment for Minor Child

I (name)_____(address)_____
(city)_____ (state)_____ (phone) _____do hereby state that I
am the natural parent or legal guardian of (child's name) _____
(age)_____ who resides with me. I authorize (name) _____ an
adult who resides at (address) _____
(city) _____ (state) _____ (phone) _____ to consent to an X-ray,
examination, anesthetic, medical or surgical diagnosis or treatment and hospital care to be
rendered to the minor child under the general or special supervision and on the advice of any
physician or surgeon licensed to practice in Indiana. I give permission to admit such visitors to
the Emergency Rooms, surgery and/or admitting that are sanctioned in the policies established by
the Board of Trustees of Columbus Regional Hospital.

Signature of Parent (s) or Guardian _____ (date) _____
Witness _____ (date) _____
Child's Doctor _____ Parent's Doctor _____

Child's Allergies to Drugs (penicillin, etc. if any) _____
Medicine Child is taking _____
Date of last Tetanus immunization _____

****

Drop Off/Pick Up Permission

My child _____, will be: (please check below)
_____ walking or riding his/her bike.
_____ I will always be dropping off and picking up my child.
Anyone except the following people listed may pick up my child from the Playground Site
_____
Emergency Phone Number (s):_____
Parent/Guardian Signature: _____

IOWA CITY RECREATION DIVISION
CONSENT FOR GIVING OF MEDICATION(S)
(Complete a separate form for each medication)

ATTENTION PARENTS AND STAFF: A NEW FORM MUST BE COMPLETED FOR EACH ACTIVITY OR SESSION AND A SEPARATE FORM MUST BE COMPLETED FOR EACH MEDICATION.
(when in doubt, ask your supervisor)

Date: _____

Child's Name _____

Physician's Name _____   Physician's Phone _____

Name of Medication _____

Please give the above medication as directed below; LIST ONLY DOSES TO BE GIVEN BY RECREATION DIVISION STAFF:

Amount to be given: _____ x _____ Doses or times per day

At what times given: _____

Number of days to be given: _____

Method of administration: _____

I (we) the undersigned parent(s)/guardian(s), give our consent to the City of Iowa City to administer the prescribed medication in the amount and method stated above.

I (we) hereby acknowledge that the service being provided is solely for the convenience of the recipient, that such service will be provided by a person who is not a health professional; however, nevertheless I(we) agree to indemnify, defend and hold harmless the City of Iowa City, its officers, agents, and employees, and Recreation Division staff, from any and all claims, damages, costs, charges, expenses and suits arising or resulting from the giving or failure to give medications as provided above.

Signed _____   Dated _____

Record of Medication

Name of Child _____

Name of Medication _____

DATE	AMOUNT	TIME GIVEN	INITIAL OF STAFF (signed when given)	DATE	AMOUNT	TIME GIVEN	INITIAL OF STAFF (signed when given)

All nonprescription and prescription medications require a written parental authorization. Each prescription shall be clearly labeled with the child's name, physician's name, name of medication, dosage and time medication is to be given. Non-prescription medications shall be in the original container and labeled with the child's name. For long-term medication, do not send more than a supply for the session or activity (maximum two weeks).

Employee Guide for Work-Related Injuries and Illnesses

When Injured At Work

If you are injured at work, notify your supervisor as soon as you can. He or she can assist you in the proper submission of your worker's compensation claim.

Call the HealthPartners CareLine Service for information about where to get treatment.

If you are hospitalized and unable to notify CareLine, your supervisor must notify the HealthPartners case manager as soon as possible.

CareLine
(952) 883-5484 or
1-888-544-5484 Toll-free

HealthPartners CareLine staff of specially trained nurses is available 24-hours-a-day, seven days a week. They will provide medical care instructions and refer you when necessary to the most appropriate clinics.

These nurses will use the following guidelines when helping you receive care:

- If emergency care is needed, call 911.
- If medical care is needed immediately, first aid instructions will be given prior to seeing a primary care provider.
- Assist in scheduling an appointment within 24 hours at either one of the HealthPartners select sites for initial assessment and evaluation, or your own primary care provider, if that is what you choose. You will be informed of your choices by the CareLine nurses.

Although we encourage you to take advantage of the CareLine Service, you can also access the health care system to receive an initial evaluation in the following ways:

- Direct access (walk in) to the clinic
- Phone to the clinic for an appointment
- Direct access to the emergency room or urgent care facility.

If you would like to receive a copy of the HealthPartners WCMCP network directory, contact the HealthPartners WCMCP administrative office telephone number listed in this brochure.

Where to Go for Medical Treatment

Initial Evaluation
If your employer has elected a HealthPartners WCMCP designated clinic for your initial evaluation, you or the CareLine nurse may schedule an appointment for you there. Your designated clinic information is located in box on other side of this brochure. You will be seen within 24 hours.

You are required to receive services from a HealthPartners WCMCP network provider except in the following circumstance:

- In an emergency
- If you have a documented history of treatment (before the injury) with a health care provider who maintains your medical records. You must, within 10 calendar days of reporting the injury to your employer, provide HealthPartners with copies of medical records or a letter from the health care provider documenting the dates of the previous treatment. However, if you change doctors, it must be to a doctor within the managed care plan.
- If your place of employment and residence is located more than 30 miles from a HealthPartners WCMCP network provider, if you live or work within the seven-county metropolitan area, or more than 50 miles if you live or work outside the metro area.
- If you are referred by HealthPartners WCMCP to a non-network provider.
- If you had an injury prior to the effective date of the managed care plan, you may continue to receive treatment from your non-network provider until you change doctors.

Follow Up Care
You may continue to see the provider who performs your initial evaluation, or you may choose to see another HealthPartners WCMCP network provider for follow up care. You may also choose to see a non-network provider with whom you have an established relationship. You must call HealthPartners WCMCP case management at (952) 883-5396 any time you wish to change providers.

About the HealthPartners WCMCP Network

You may receive treatment from a HealthPartners WCMCP network primary care, occupational health, or specialty physician, chiropractor, podiatrist, osteopath, or dentist, if the treatment is within the provider's scope of practice and appropriate for your injury or illness.

HealthPartners

Workers' Compensation Managed Care Plan

Employee Guide for Work-Related Injuries and Illnesses

Designated Clinic

Your employer has selected the designated HealthPartners WCMCP clinic below where you should go to receive your initial evaluation:

Regions Occupational Medicine Clinic
640 Jackson Street
Saint Paul, MN 55101
(651)-254-3313

Employer Contact:

Your work place contact for worker's compensations is:

Workers Compensation Staff
Risk Management
Human Resources Department
City of Saint Paul
651-266-6500

Important Telephone Numbers

CareLine
952 - 883-5484   Metro
1-888-544-5484   Toll-free

Call the above number 24-hours- a - day, seven days a week to receive medical care information and coordinate appointment scheduling for a work-related injury.

HealthPartners Case Manager
952-883-5396   Metro
1-888-779-3625   Toll-free

A resource for the supervisor/manager, employee, or provider to obtain assistance or discuss the treatment of an employee's injury and subsequent return to work.

HealthPartners Worker's Compensation Administrative Office
952-883-5396

Call the number above to obtain program information, dispute resolution information or copies of the HealthPartners WCMCP network directory.

Minnesota Department of Labor and Industry (Metro)
651-284-5032

Minnesota Department of Labor and Industry (Greater Minnesota)
1-800-DIAL-DLI (342-5354)

Minnesota Department of Labor and Industry (Duluth)
1-800-365-4584
or 218-723-4670

An issue which cannot be resolved within 30 days to the satisfaction of the employee may be appealed to the Minnesota Department of Labor and Industry.

Appendix E

Incident Report Forms

- Complaints Regarding Sexual Predators
- Participant/Visitor Accident Report
- Employee's Safety Report
- Supervisor's Safety Report
- Accident and Incident Reporting Procedures for Volunteers
- Work-Related Injury Procedures

**SAINT PAUL PARKS AND RECREATION
Policy and Procedures - DIVISION**

NUMBER: DIV.6.2.2   **EFFECTIVE DATE:** 1/1/2003

SUBJECT: **GUIDELINES FOR HANDLING COMPLAINTS REGARDING SEXUAL PREDATORS**

PURPOSE: Instructions for staff for handling complaints regarding sexual predators.
PROCEDURES:

***Call the police** if it is a direct complaint from a visitor (witness) and the suspect is on-site.

    Police: 911 or 651-291-1111 (non emergency)

***Monitor the suspect** - assign another staff person, or someone you trust to monitor the behaviors and location of the suspect. Keep the number of people monitoring the suspect to a minimum, so as not to raise suspicion with the suspect.

***Tell** the dispatcher you have a complaint from a visitor (witness) regarding a suspected sexual predator that **MAY** currently be on site. Tell the dispatcher you have someone monitoring the suspect. Dispatch will most likely want to talk to the visitor (witness).

***Ask** the visitor (witness) to wait in the office for the police to arrive.
The police will need the visitor (witness) to identify the suspect and make a statement. Without this we are not able to prosecute.

It is **NOT necessary to get personal information from the visitor (witness) if they wish to remain anonymous. The police will get the information they need from the visitor (witness) when they arrive.

Get the following information: from the visitor (witness) and the Police:

1.   **Description** of the suspect from head-to-toe. Height/body build; hair color; Accessories such as a hat, glasses, jewelry ; Facial hair and features; Clothing styles and colors, Shoe style and color.

2.   **Location of the suspect.**
   - Where were they last seen?
   - Which direction did they go?
   - Traveling on foot or vehicle?
   - Make/model/color of vehicle?
   - License Plate (state & number)
   - Moving fast or slow?
   - How long ago?
   -

3.   Contact your supervisor. They need to know the details of the situation.

4.   Document the complaint and all your actions in an Incident Report (who, what, where, when, why).

5.   Police report Case Number (CN#), officer name, badge and squad number.

Page 1 of 2

SAINT PAUL PARKS AND RECREATION
Policy and Procedures - DIVISION

REQUIRED ITEMS AND/OR RELATED INFORMATION:

SECTION MANAGER'S RESPONSIBILITIES	SUPERVISOR'S RESPONSIBILITIES	EMPLOYEE'S RESPONSIBILITIES
Ensure all employees under his/her jurisdiction are aware of this policy and procedures. Ensure that supervisors in his/her section enforce this policy and procedures.	Advise all employees of this policy and procedures. Ensure that employees follow this policy and procedures. Issue warnings or initiate disciplinary action as needed to ensure employee compliance.	Adhere to the policy. Follow the procedures. Ask for additional training if needed.

Owner: Eric Thompson, Park Security   **Next Review Date:** 12/08

CITY OF SAINT PAUL

No 13585

DIVISION OF
PARKS AND RECREATION

PARTICIPANT/VISITOR ACCIDENT REPORT

NAME OF ACCIDENT VICTIM _____ AGE _____

ADDRESS _____ PHONE NO.: _____

FACILITY SITE, ADDRESS, PHONE NO. _____

DATE OF ACCIDENT _____ TIME OF ACCIDENT _____

TYPE OF INJURY (DESCRIPTION) _____

_____

TREATMENT ADMINISTERED _____

_____

_____

TREATMENT RECOMMENDED: DOCTOR _____   PARAMEDICS _____   HOSPITAL _____

EXPLAIN CIRCUMSTANCES OF ACCIDENT IN DETAIL - USE OTHER SIDE IF NECESSARY

_____

_____

OTHER PARTIES INVOLVED: WITNESSES _____

NAME _____ ADDRESS _____

RELATIONSHIP _____

NAME _____ ADDRESS _____

RELATIONSHIP _____

EMPLOYEE ADMINISTERING FIRST AID - NAME: _____ DATE _____

ADDRESS _____ PHONE_____

EMPLOYEES ON DUTY _____

_____

PERSON IN CHARGE OF PREMISES _____

I HAVE READ AND UNDERSTAND THIS REPORT (SIGNATURE OF ACCIDENT VICTIM OR GUARDIAN)

_____

SEND TO PARKS AND RECREATION ADMINISTRATION OFFICE, 300 CITY HALL ANNEX

DISTRIBUTION: White-CA; Yellow-Rec. File; Pink-Admin. File; gldrd-Facility File

4-92

CITY OF SAINT PAUL

EMPLOYEE'S SAFETY REPORT

INJURY OR AGGRAVATION

EMPLOYEE MUST SUBMIT THIS REPORT WITHIN 24 HOURS OF WORK-RELATED INJURY OR AGGRAVATION.

DEPARTMENT_____ DIVISION_____ ACTIVITY CODE_____

1 Name of injured employee_____ Phone: Home_____ Work_____

2 Home address (including city and zip code)_____

3 Date of Birth_____ ☐ Male ☐ Female Marital status_____ Soc. Sec. #_____

4 Job title_____ Salary $_____ ☐ Hourly ☐ Biweekly

5 Job Status ☐ Full time ☐ Part time ☐ Temporary Do you have another job? ☐ No ☐ Yes

6 If YES, provide company name, your position and salary: _____

INJURY INFORMATION

7 Date injured_____ Time_____ Date reported to supervisor_____ Was time lost from work? ☐ No ☐ Yes

First day lost (date)_____ Return to work, actual or expected (date)_____

8 Was medical treatment given? ☐ No ☐ Yes Provide name and address of physician and/or hospital:

9 Nature of injury (cut, sprain, burn, etc.)_____

10 Part/parts of body injured_____

11 Exact location of accident_____

12 Describe accident in detail_____

13 If aggravation, what caused resumption of symptoms?_____

14 Did you have a prior injury to this portion of the body? ☐ No ☐ Yes When?_____

Did prior injury or disability contribute to this injury? ☐ No ☐ Yes Explain?_____

15 Witnesses (names and phone numbers)_____

I certify that all statements in this report are true. _____ Date_____
(Employee Signature)

Supervisor's comments: _____

Supervisor's signature: _____

WHITE--Workers' Compensation Administrator   YELLOW--Department   PINK--Supervisor

CITY OF SAINT PAUL

SUPERVISOR'S SAFETY REPORT

INJURY OR AGGRAVATION

> **THIS FORM MUST BE COMPLETED** by the supervisor for each work-related injury or aggravation within 24 hours.

DEPARTMENT_____ DIVISION_____ACTIVITY CODE_____

1 Name of injured employee_____

2 Date of Injury_____ Was time lost from work?   ☐ Yes   ☐ No

3 Was site of injury visited?   ☐ Yes   ☐ No   Date of site visit_____

4 What can be done to prevent a similar occurrence?_____
_____

5 Was any corrective action taken?   ☐ No   ☐ Yes--Describe_____
_____
_____

6 Did another person, tools, or equipment contribute to this injury?   ☐ No   ☐ Yes--Identify and describe how_____
_____
_____

7 Was safety equipment available?   ☐ No   ☐ Yes   ☐ Does not apply

8 Was safety equipment in use?   ☐ No   ☐ Yes   ☐ Does not apply

9 At the time of the injury, how many hours had the employee been working?_____

10 If injury occurred outdoors, describe the weather conditions at the time_____
_____

YOUR ROLE IN A SPEEDY RETURN-TO-WORK IS OF UTMOST IMPORTANCE. IF ABSENCE FROM WORK EXCEEDS THREE CALENDAR DAYS, PERSONAL CONTACT IS WARRANTED.

A. Ask about recovery status and progress.

B. Is employee satisfied with medical care to date?

C. Does employee have any questions?

D. What is estimated return-to-work date?

E. Assure employee that his/her job is not in jeopardy because of injury, and that you and co-workers are anxious for employee's return-to-work. Find out if light-duty will speed return-to-work.

F. Discuss other pertinent issues and questions.

Follow-up calls should take place every week until return-to-work.

Information obtained from employees should be shared with departmental Workers' Compensation liaison and the City's Workers' Compensation staff at (651) 266-6500.

If you or the employee have any questions, please call the Workers' Compensation staff at (651) 266-6500.

---

11 Any additional information regarding the case_____
_____
_____
_____

Supervisor's Name_____ Supervisor's Phone_____

Supervisor's Signature_____ Date_____

WHITE--Workers' Compensation Administrator   YELLOW--Department   PINK--Supervisor

SAINT PAUL PARKS AND RECREATION
Policy and Procedures - DIVISION

NUMBER: DIV.3.3.3   **EFFECTIVE DATE:** 1996

Revised Date: 01/06

SUBJECT. **ACCIDENT AND INCIDENT REPORTING PROCEDURES FOR VOLUNTEERS**

PURPOSE: Volunteers contributing their time to the City of St. Paul are covered by the City against damages resulting from their actions.

In order to protect both the volunteer and the City, proper procedures must be followed in the event of an accident or incident which could result in liability for damages.

PROCEDURES:

(Any question of when a report should be filled out can be answered by the site or program supervisor.)

1. In the event of an accident, administer only the first aid that you are trained to give. Do not try to do more than your knowledge permits. If necessary, do not hesitate to call the Paramedics for injury treatment.

2. Any accident requiring treatment necessitates a Division of Parks and Recreation Participant/Visitor Accident Report being filled out. This report must be turned into the Division's downtown office within 24 hours of any serious accident. These reports are immediately turned over to the City Attorney's Office. If there are weather or site conditions, or other influences on the accident, also fill out a Confidential File Memo in addition to the Accident Report.

3. If you are contacted by an attorney or other representative of the person involved in the accident or incident, refer any and all contacts to the Saint Paul City Attorney's Office, 400 City Hall, 266-8710. Do not speak to any representative yourself.

4. Our staff is familiar with all procedures followed in the case of an accident. They will fill out the necessary reports and forms with your help.

REQUIRED ITEMS AND/OR RELATED INFORMATION:
Participant/Visitor Accident Report form
Confidential File Memo form
Incident Report form

SAINT PAUL PARKS AND RECREATION
Policy and Procedures - DIVISION

SECTION MANAGER=S RESPONSIBILITIES	SUPERVISOR=S RESPONSIBILITIES	EMPLOYEE=S RESPONSIBILITIES
Ensure all employees under his/her jurisdiction are aware of this policy and procedures.	Advise all employees of this policy and procedures.	Adhere to the policy.
Ensure that supervisors in his/her section enforce this policy and procedures.	Ensure that employees follow this policy and procedures.	Follow the procedures.
	Issue warnings or initiate disciplinary action as needed to ensure employee compliance.	Ask for additional training if needed.

Owner: Darlene McMinn
Safety Co-ordinator

Next Review Date: 01/07

Work-Related Injury Procedures

The City of Saint Paul contracts with a managed care provider, HealthPartners, for determining medical appropriateness of treatment for work-related injuries. **However, the City's Risk Management Division will determine if your Workers' Compensation claim will be approved.** As participants in the HealthPartners Workers' Compensation Managed Care Plan, employees and supervisors are to use the following steps in the event of a work-related injury:

Employees:

✔ **Call 911** immediately if the injury is life threatening. **For emergency situations**, seek medical care from any available emergency provider.

✔ For **non-emergency situations**, call **HealthPartners CareLine at 952-883-5484** (Metro) or 1-888-544-5484 (toll free). CareLine is HealthPartners' 24-hour, seven-day-a-week nurse triage line; you will speak to a nurse who will assess your injury and help coordinate a medical appointment for you within 24 hours.

✔ Report the injury to your supervisor immediately. You should obtain an Employee Guide and a Managed Care Identification Card from your supervisor. Bring your HealthPartners Managed Care ID card with you when seeking medical attention.

✔ Complete an Employee's Safety Report **within 24 hours** of the injury and submit it to your supervisor. This report must be completed for **all** injuries, even if no medical attention was necessary and/or there was no time lost from work.

✔ If medical attention is necessary, you must receive that care from a HealthPartners provider, preferably:
Regions Occupational Medicine Clinic
640 Jackson Street
St. Paul, MN 55101
651-254-3313
Monday - Friday 8:00 a.m. - 5:00 p.m.

If you choose not to use the Regions Occupational Medicine Clinic, a complete list of all HealthPartners providers is available by calling HealthPartners at 952-883-5396. You may see your own doctor instead of a HealthPartners provider **only** if you have seen that doctor twice within the past two years. **Important**: You must seek medical support on your **first** day of lost time from work. Urgent situations may be seen on a "walk-in" basis at the above provider.

✔ Upon arrival at the clinic, show your HealthPartners Managed Care ID card to clinic personnel and inform them that you are a participant in HealthPartners Managed Care. **This is for work-related injuries only.** After each clinic visit, you must obtain a Work Ability form. Return this form to your supervisor immediately.

✔ Remind the doctor that all tests and procedures (e.g., hospital admission, surgery, MRIs, etc.) must be pre-approved by HealthPartners, or they might not be paid. **Important:** Tell the provider or pharmacy that **all** bills for work-related injuries **must** be sent to the HealthPartners, Work Comp Claims, PO Box 1277, Minneapolis, MN 55440-1277.

✔ **Please note:** If your injury occurs during an evening shift or on the weekend, the following clinics have extended office hours:

HealthPartners Saint Paul Urgent Care	Regions Hospital - Emergency Room
205 Wabasha Street; St. Paul	640 Jackson Street; St. Paul
612-339-3663	651-221-3456
Mon-Fri 5:00-9:30 p.m.; Sat/Sun 10:00 a.m.-9:30 p.m.	24 hours a day/7 days a week

✔ If follow-up care is necessary after the initial evaluation, you have three options: 1) Continue to treat with the initial evaluating HealthPartners provider; 2) Treat with any other provider in the HealthPartners Workers' Compensation network; or 3) Document an established relationship with a provider outside the HealthPartners Workers' Compensation network. When you choose the last option, you must call the HealthPartners Case Manager at 952-883-5396.

✔ The law allows an employee to change providers during treatment. Changing from the initial evaluating provider is not considered a change of provider. To change, the employee must select a provider from within the HealthPartners Workers' Compensation network (unless you have documented an established relationship). Any time a change of providers is made, the HealthPartners Case Manager must be notified.

✔ Contact the City's Risk Management Division at 651-266-6500 if you have any questions about work-related injuries, Workers' Compensation, or these procedures.

✔ If you have any questions about the HealthPartners Workers' Compensation Managed Care Plan, or treatment for your illness or injury, please contact a HealthPartners Case Manager or the Administrative Office at 952-883-5396.

Work-Related Injury Procedures - page 2

Supervisors:

✔ Provide all new employees with information about how to report work-related injuries by giving employees an Employee Notification Letter and an Employee Guide. **This is REQUIRED BY LAW.** Extra Employee Guides are available from HealthPartners at 952-883-7574. Train your staff about what to do if an employee is injured; review the process with them.

✔ Display the Managed Care Plan posters in an area that can be seen by all of your employees. **This is REQUIRED BY LAW.**

✔ At the time of injury, provide the employee with an Employee Guide and a HealthPartners Managed Care ID card, and remind employees to show their ID card to clinic personnel. Tell them they must obtain a Work Ability form from the doctor at each visit.

✔ For non-emergency work-related injuries requiring medical attention, encourage employees to go to Regions Occupational Medicine Clinic for care. If an employee chooses not to go to the Regions Occupational Medicine Clinic, provide the employee with a list of other medical providers. You can obtain a directory from HealthPartners by calling 952-883-5484.

✔ If the injury occurs during an evening shift or on the weekend, refer employees to the facilities listed on the other side of this sheet.

✔ **Important:** Remind employees to inform their medical provider or pharmacy that all bills for work-related injuries **must** be submitted to the HealthPartners, Work Comp Claims, PO Box 1277, Minneapolis, MN 55440-1277.

✔ Obtain a Work Ability form from the employee after each visit to a doctor and immediately send it to the Risk Management, Human Resources, 400 City Hall Annex, or fax it to Risk Management at 651-266-8886.

✔ Review the Work Ability form with the employee to ensure that both you and the employee understand any restrictions, treatments, referrals, and follow-up plans. A Case Manager from HealthPartners will track and monitor all work-related injuries. They will work with you and the provider to facilitate the injured worker's prompt and safe return to work. You may be called by a Case Manager to discuss an employee's progress and short or long-term job options. You may contact the Case Manager at any time with questions or concerns about the injured employee's medical status and return-to-work capabilities by calling 952-883-5396.

✔ **Important:** Employees must seek medical support on their **first** day of lost time from work. Urgent situations can be seen on a "walk-in" basis at Regions Occupational Medicine Clinic.

✔ If an employee is injured on the job, you must do the following **within 24 hours**, even if no medical attention was necessary and/or there was no time lost from work:

　✔ Complete a First Report of Injury form and immediately fax it to HealthPartners at 952-883-5210. Send the original to the Risk Management, Human Resources, 400 City Hall Annex. This report is to be completed by the supervisor or department liaison, **not** by the injured employee. The only form the employee completes is the Employee's Safety Report.

　✔ Complete a Supervisor's Safety Report. Send the green and blue copies to the Risk Management, Human Resources, 400 City Hall Annex; give the pink copy to your department director; and retain the goldenrod copy for your files.

　✔ Obtain the Employee's Safety Report from the injured employee. Send the white and canary copies to the Risk Management, Human Resources, 400 City Hall Annex; give the pink copy to your department director; and retain the goldenrod copy for your files.

　Please note: You can obtain additional blank report forms from the Risk Management Division by calling 651-266-6500.

✔ Maintain a positive relationship with the injured employee, establish a safe return-to-work setting, and communicate effectively with all involved parties.

✔ Fatal accidents, or accidents where 3 or more employees are hospitalized, must be reported to Minnesota OSHA **within 8 hours** by calling 651-284-5050. If incident occurs outside of business hours, report incident to Federal OSHA at 1-800-321-OSHA.

✔ Please contact the City's Risk Management staff, Human Resources at 651-266-6500 if you have any questions about work-related injuries, Workers' Compensation, or these procedures.

Risk Management, Human Resources   June 2004

Appendix F

Evaluations, Inclement Weather, Protecting Crime Scenes

- Special Event Evaluation
- Coaching Evaluation Form
- Umpire Evaluation Form
- Event Planning for Undesirable Weather
- Crime Scenes–Protecting the Area

COLUMBUS PARKS AND RECREATION DEPARTMENT

SPECIAL EVENT EVALUATION
Please return to Donner Center Office

Name   of   Event_____Date_____

Please help us evaluate and improve our services by answering the questions below. Your feedback is important to our operation and to the improvement of future events.

Rating

	Poor				Excellent

Security Issues

	Poor				Excellent
Was there adequate security staff scheduled?	1	2	3	4	5
Was the crowd control operation adequate?	1	2	3	4	5

Please communicate the success and concerns you
observed with the security operation.

Vending Sales

	Poor				Excellent
Was there an adequate number and type of vendors?	1	2	3	4	5
Were the locations of the vendors adequate?	1	2	3	4	5

Please communicate the success and concerns you
observed with the vending operation.

Parking

	Poor				Excellent
Was there adequate parking available?	1	2	3	4	5
Was the parking sinage adequate?	1	2	3	4	5
Was there adequate parking control personnel?	1	2	3	4	5
Was there adequate parking for the physically challenged?	1	2	3	4	5

Please communicate the success and concerns you
observed with the parking operation?

Maintenance Support Services

	Poor				Excellent
Was the number of clean-up staff scheduled for the event?	1	2	3	4	5
Was the garbage disposal system adequate for the event?	1	2	3	4	5
Were the restroom facilities adequate?	1	2	3	4	5
Were the restroom facilities clean?	1	2	3	4	5

Please communcate the success and concerns you observed
with the maintenance support operation.

Columbus Babe Ruth - Parks & Recreation
Coaching Evaluation Form
(To be completed by each Umpire)

Date:_____   Diamond #:_____

Coach #1 (Last Name): _____   Team #1: _____

Coach #2 (Last Name):_____   Team #2: _____

Form completed by Umpire

Base Umpire: ___   Plate Umpire: ___

> **Please complete the following section by circling the appropriate number.**
> **(1-5, 5 being the best)**

Coach #1

Measurement	Rating	Comments (If Any)
Appearance	1 2 3 4 5	_____
Positive interaction with Players	1 2 3 4 5	_____
Positive interaction with You (Umpire)	1 2 3 4 5	_____
Organization (Smooth running game)	1 2 3 4 5	_____

Coach #2

Measurement	Rating	Comments (If Any)
Appearance	1 2 3 4 5	_____
Positive interaction with Players	1 2 3 4 5	_____
Positive interaction with You (Umpire)	1 2 3 4 5	_____
Organization (Smooth running game)	1 2 3 4 5	_____

department of
PARKS
&REC

UMPIRE EVALUATION FORM

Umpire _____

Site _____ Date _____

Evaluator_____

Performance:

Plate Work

	Unacceptable		Meets Standards		Outstanding
Stability of Head and Body Position	1	2	3	4	5
Timing	1	2	3	4	5
Proper Positioning for plays	1	2	3	4	5
Style and Mechanics of calls	1	2	3	4	5
Consistency of Strike Zone throughout the game	1	2	3	4	5
Judgement and Interpretation of Strike Zone	1	2	3	4	5
Crew Mechanics (if applicable)	N/A 1	2	3	4	5
Crew Communications	N/A 1	2	3	4	5

Base Work (if applicable)

	Unacceptable		Meets Standards		Outstanding
Timing	1	2	3	4	5
Proper Positioning of Calls	1	2	3	4	5
Style and Mechanics of Calls	1	2	3	4	5
Judgement Calls	1	2	3	4	5
Crew Mechanics	1	2	3	4	5
Reaction to Development of Plays	1	2	3	4	5

Game & Situation Management

	Unacceptable		Meets Standards		Outstanding
Policies and Procedures	1	2	3	4	5
Playing Rules	1	2	3	4	5
Situation Management/Ejections	1	2	3	4	5

Effort & Professionalism

	Unacceptable		Meets Standards		Outstanding
Focus	1	2	3	4	5
Hustle	1	2	3	4	5
Demeanor	1	2	3	4	5
Appearance	1	2	3	4	5
Mobility	1	2	3	4	5
Fraternization	1	2	3	4	5

***Ratings of 2 or lower should be accompanied by specific comments on next page.

Indy Parks and Recreation

Event Planning for Undesirable Weather

Event organizers have the responsibility to plan for and address weather safety concerns for all event attendees. Proper planning will prepare organizers in knowing what action to take if undesirable weather is present during their event. This may include thunder, lightning, excessive heat or cold, and precipitation, not to mention fast moving storms that may or may not be severe. It is important to keep these factors in mind while planning any event, regardless of size. Listed below are some questions that may aid in the planning process.

1. What steps will be taken to safe guard attendees if lightning and/or thunder is present?
2. Under what circumstances will event attendees be asked to take shelter?
3. Where is adequate shelter in relationship to the event and how long will it take to get attendees into the shelter?
4. How and who will monitor incoming weather?
5. How will information be disseminated to all those involved with the event?
6. Can mitigation help in reducing the hazards of undesirable weather (i.e. holding events early in the day to reduce heat stress)?

Planning for weather should also include other factors beside event attendees. Other questions that should be asked when planning events:

1. What are the wind limits of large tents?
2. If smaller tents are present what will be done to keep them from being picked up by the wind.
3. How will the wind affect banners, start lines, stage lights, etc.?

May 12, 2004   1

4. In the event of precipitation, are power cords connected to ground fault circuit interrupters?

Other hazards to consider:
1. Power lines that could be brought down by a severe storm.
2. Structures and equipment prone to lighting strikes
3. Waterways that may be prone to flooding. Flash flooding is the nation's number one weather killer after heat. Streams, ditches or culverts may become un-crossable in the event of heavy rains.
4. Areas, including off-road parking, that may be susceptible to brush and/or grass fires during dry periods.
5. High winds.
6. Snow removal.

It is our hope that event organizers will take the time to plan and prepare for undesirable weather to ensure safety for all those involved with their special events at Indy Parks. To help with your awareness of weather hazards and recommended courses of action, consider the National Weather Service (NWS) websites listed below:

For NWS forecasts and warnings: http://www.crh.noaa.gov/ind/ (click on the map for the Indy Park you'll be at).

For NWS radar data: http://www.crh.noaa.gov/radar/latest/DS.p19r0/si.kind.shtml (click your refresh button for the most recent radar image).

For more information on lightning safety see: http://www.lightningsafety.noaa.gov

For more on flood safety see: http://www.srh.weather.gov/tadd/

For storm safety see: http://www.srh.noaa.gov/oun/severewx/safety.html#tornado
For a simple NWS web reference, see: www.weather.gov (click on the desired location on the map)

May 12, 2004   2

Risk Management Policies - 6070

Date: January 25, 2000   **Accreditation Standard #: 8.3.2**

POLICY RE: **Crime Scenes – Protecting the Area**

The following should assist in the understanding of what physical evidence is, and how it is used in a criminal investigation. With this knowledge it should be much easier to identify and protect a crime scene.

What is a crime scene?

1. Any place where a crime has occurred or where any type of physical evidence is left or deposited.

2. Almost anything can be evidence.

What can physical evidence do for a criminal investigation?

1. Identification
    a. First step is to identify the evidence.
    b. Drugs, arson accelerando, bloodstains are examples of evidence that have to be identified.

2. Individualization
    a. Demonstration that a particular sample is unique, even among members of the same class; example, shoe print that has a cut in the heel.
    b. Can also show that evidence came from a common source; example, broken chrome off of a suspect vehicle.
    c. Personal identification; example, fingerprints, DNA and bite marks.

3. Reconstruction
    a. Putting the pieces together to gain an understanding of past events from the physical evidence; example, automobile accident.

What can physical evidence reveal?

1. Information on Corpus Delicti (body of the crime).
    a. Tool marks, broken doors or windows, ransacked rooms and missing valuables are evidence that are needed to prove burglary.
    b. A weapon, blood, torn clothing are all evidence that can be used in an assault case.

2. Information on the Modus Operandi (method of operation).
    a. Many criminals have a particular method of committing a crime.
    b. Items that are taken may be the same.
    c. Items left at the scene.

Page 1 of 3

Bloomington
Parks and Recreation

Risk Management Policies - 6070

Date: January 25, 2000   **Accreditation Standard #: 8.3.2**

3. Linking a suspect with a victim.
    a.   This type of evidence is very important.
    b.   Especially true in violent crimes.
    c.   Blood, hairs, clothing fibers and cosmetics may be transferred from the suspect to the victim.
    d.   Items found with the suspect may link the suspect to the crime scene - such as a knife with the victim's blood on the knife.
    e.   Victim's and suspect's clothing need to be protected for trace evidence.

4. Linking a person to a crime scene.
    a.   This is evidence left at the crime scene by the suspect.
    b.   Examples are fingerprints, glove prints, blood, semen, cartridge cases, tool marks, foot prints, tire tracks.

5. Disproving or supporting a witness' testimony.
    a.   Under stress a witness may not see things as they actually happened.
    b.   Can help in proving if the victim is lying.

6. Identification of a suspect.
    a.   Main goal of physical evidence.
    b.   Fingerprints, DNA, bite marks.

7. Providing investigative leads.
    a.   Such as in a hit-and-run case, paint chips will show you the color of a car.

Crime Scenes that Parks & Recreation May Encounter

Because of the makeup of the park and recreation program, park employees may encounter or discover almost any kind of crime. The following will cover the most common crimes.

1. Burglary
    a.   Finger prints, tools either brought by suspect or used by the suspect, items left by the suspect, items moved by the suspect, footprints.

2. Assaults
    a.   Was a weapon used & where is the weapon?
    b.   Protect clothing of victim, if the clothing is removed.
    c.   Is there a scene? Blood spatter?
    d.   Did suspect leave anything?

Bloomington
Parks and Recreation

Risk Management Policies - 6070

Date: **January 25, 2000**   **Accreditation Standard #: 8.3.2**

3. Robbery
   a. Did suspect touch anything?
   b. Did suspect leave anything?
   c. Area of retreat by suspect.

4. Rape
   a. Do not let victim take a shower or change clothing.
   b. Clothing, if removed, should be protected and not moved if possible.
   c. Did suspect leave any items?
   d. If possible, victim should not drink anything.

5. Arson
   a. Gas cans, matches, items left by suspect.
   b. Do not walk around in burnt area if possible.

6. Murder/Suicides
   a. Call for medics if there is any chance victim is still alive.
   b. Do not move victim if at all possible.
   c. Do not move any type of weapon, if possible.
   d. On a hanging suicide, if possible, do not cut the ligature.
   e. If you have to cut the ligature, cut in the long section, not near knot.
   f. Look for any suicide notes lying in the area.
   g. Keep people as far away as possible.
   h. Cover footprints/fingerprints, with a trash can.

<u>Witnesses</u>

1. Try to keep all witnesses at the scene, until the police officer arrives.
2. On the more serious crimes get the witnesses away from the crowd.
3. Keep witnesses separated if possible.
4. If a witness has to leave before police officers arrive, get their name – check identification.
5. If a parks and recreation employee should witness a crime:
   - Stay calm.
   - Immediately write down description of suspect or vehicles.

Bloomington
Parks and Recreation

The appendices A-F were reprinted by the generosity of the following agencies:

Bloomington Department of Parks and Recreation, Bloomington, IN
Champaign County Forest Preserve District, Mahomet, IL
Cleveland Metroparks, Cleveland, OH
Columbus Department of Parks and Recreation, Columbus, IN
Corpus Christi Parks and Recreation Department, Corpus Christi, TX
Foster City Department of Parks, Recreation and Vehicles, Foster City, CA
Indy Parks and Recreation, Indianapolis, IN
Iowa City Department of Parks and Recreation, Iowa City, IA
Joliet Park District, Joliet, IL
Lake County Forest Preserve District, Libertyville, IL
Long Beach Department of Parks, Recreation and Marine, Long Beach, CA
Maryland-National Capital Park and Planning Commission, Silver Springs, MD
Monmouth County Park System, Lincroft, NJ
St. Louis County Parks, St. Louis, MO
St. Paul, Minnesota Division of Parks and Recreation, St. Paul, MN

Appendix G

Occupational Safety & Health Administration, U.S. Department of Labor

OSHA'S MISSION

The mission of the Occupational Safety and Health Administration (OSHA) is to save lives, prevent injuries, and protect the health of American workers. To accomplish this, federal and state governments must work in partnership with the more than 100 million working men and women and their six and a half million employers who are covered by the Occupational Safety and Health Act of 1970.

OSHA'S SERVICES

OSHA and its state partners have approximately 2,100 inspectors, plus complaint discrimination investigators, engineers, physicians, educators, standard writers, and other technical and support personnel spread over more than 200 offices throughout the country. This staff establishes protective standards, enforces those standards, and reaches out to employers and employees through technical assistance and consultation programs.

OSHA'S CONSULTATION DIRECTORY

OSHA maintains an active website Consultation Director at http://www.osha.gov/oshinfo/mission.html. *This website includes all 50 states, the District of Columbia, Guam, Puerto Rico, and the Virgin Islands. You will find phone numbers, E-mail addresses, and individual websites for each location.*

Appendix H

Sources of Additional Information on Establishing Risk-Management Programs

PARK DISTRICT RISK MANAGEMENT AGENCY (PDRMA)

PDRMA'S Mission

The mission of PDRMA is to sustain a partnership of park and recreation agencies committed to providing a safer environment to work and play through effective management of human and financial resources.

Public Entity Risk Pooling

In 1973, the Illinois General Assembly passed legislation that enabled public entities to combine together to meet their risk management and insurance needs. This type of organization became known as a public entity pool. The first Illinois pool was organized in 1979.

This legislation proved to be visionary. In the mid to late 1980s, the "insurance crisis" hit Illinois. Public entities found themselves being cancelled by commercial insurers. From 1984 to 1988, park and recreation agencies saw insurance limits decrease over 700% while the cost increased 850% or more. Everyone said, "There must be a better way!"

In 1984, the Park District Risk Management Agency (PDRMA) was created by park and recreation agencies as an alternative to commercial insurance. The organization's purpose was to combine resources to pay losses, purchase insurance, develop risk management and loss control programs, and defend lawsuits brought against the members.

In the years since its founding, public entity pooling has become widespread. Pools exist in almost every state and recent industry studies show that alternative risk financing programs such as this account for over 30% of the property and liability insurance market, representing over 50 billion dollars annually.

To find out more about PDRMA's extensive program of creating partnerships, their means of controlling claims, in-house services, and consultation, plus much more, visit their website at **http://www.pdrma.org.**

PUBLIC AGENCY RISK MANAGERS ASSOCIATION (PARMA)

PARMA is a forum that promotes, develops, and facilitates education and leadership in public agency risk management.

PARMA's vision includes the empowerment of risk management practitioners through education, training, and information exchange in all relevant areas, including:
>   Property and liability
>   Worker's compensation
>   Employee relations and benefits
>   Safety and loss prevention
>   Financial risk

PARMA is a California not-for-profit corporation with over 400 public entity members and over 200 associate members. As we as an annual conference, the five regional chapters provide periodical local training sessions for their members covering issues in liability, worker's compensation, property, employee benefits, and loss prevention. For additional information, contact their website at *http://www.parma.com*.

Index